Stepping Out Theatre in Associatic
and Simon James Collier presents

Lullabies of Broadmoor
– A Broadmoor Quartet
by Steve Hennessy

The Corner House, Frome 12–13 July 2011
The Alma Tavern Theatre, Bristol 19–23 July 2011
The Nightingale Theatre, Brighton 25–26 July 2011
C venues, Edinburgh Festival Fringe, 3–27 August 2011
Finborough Theatre, London, 30 August–1 October 2011

Wilderness was commissioned and first produced by Theatre West in October 2002.
The Murder Club was first produced by Theatre West in November 2003.
The Demon Box was commissioned and first produced by Theatre West in November 2007.
Venus at Broadmoor was commissioned and first produced by Theatre West in November 2010.

FINBOROUGH | THEATRE

The Murder Club was originally commissioned by the Finborough Theatre.
The Murder Club and *Wilderness* were first produced in London at the Finborough Theatre in 2004.
The Demon Box received a staged reading at the Finborough Theatre
as part of *Vibrant – An Anniversary Festival of Finborough Playwrights* on Friday, 18 June 2010.

Lullabies of Broadmoor – A Broadmoor Quartet

by Steve Hennessy

Cast in alphabetical order

Venus at Broadmoor

Dr. Orange	**Chris Bianchi**
Dr. Beard	**Chris Courtenay**
John Coleman	**Chris Donnelly**
Christiana Edmunds	**Violet Ryder**

The Demon Box

Richard Dadd	**Chris Bianchi**
William Chester Minor	**Chris Courtenay**
John Coleman	**Chris Donnelly**
Ariel	**Violet Ryder**

The Murder Club

Ronald True	**Chris Bianchi**
Richard Prince	**Chris Courtenay**
John Coleman	**Chris Donnelly**
Olive Young	**Violet Ryder**

Wilderness

George Merrett	**Chris Bianchi**
William Chester Minor	**Chris Courtenay**
John Coleman	**Chris Donnelly**
Eliza Merrett	**Violet Ryder**

Director	**Chris Loveless**
Set Designer	**Ann Stiddard**
Lighting Designer	**Tim Bartlett**
Costume Designer	**Rebecca Sellors**

Venus at Broadmoor is dedicated to Sidney Barker (1867–1871)

The Demon Box is dedicated to Robert Dadd (1789–1843)

The Murder Club is dedicated to Olive Young (1897–1922)
and William Terriss (1847–1897)

Wilderness is dedicated to George Merrett (? – 1872)

Production Acknowledgements
Movement Director | **Cheryl Douglas**
Fight Director | **Chris Donnelly**
Press Representative | **Finborough Theatre 07977 173135**

Each play lasts approximately 65 minutes.

There will be one interval of fifteen minutes between each play.

Our patrons are respectfully reminded that, in this intimate theatre, any noise such as rustling programmes, talking or the ringing of mobile phones may distract the actors and your fellow audience-members.

This production is supported by

Foreword

Steve Hennessy, Playwright, *Lullabies of Broadmoor*

When I wrote a play about a well-known 19th-century resident of Broadmoor Criminal Lunatic Asylum back in 2002, I had no idea I was about to embark on a project that would stretch across almost a decade. My interest in the subject matter, as for many of my plays, came partly from a background working in mental health. Since 1997 I had also been running Stepping Out Theatre, a mental health theatre group producing large-scale community plays with mental health service users and small-scale studio productions with professional actors on mental health themes.

With Chester Minor as its subject, *Wilderness*, the first Broadmoor play to be written, was produced in Bristol that year. I sent it to Neil McPherson, Artistic Director of the Finborough Theatre, who helpfully suggested the subject matter for a second play about another well-known Broadmoor patient and *The Murder Club* duly followed in 2003. It featured Ronald True, a small time conman who had murdered a woman just down the road from the Finborough Theatre before winding up in Broadmoor. *The Murder Club* was written in the year that British forces participated in the American invasion of Iraq, and it was set during an earlier British occupation of Iraq in 1922. Researching the echoes between the two events fascinated me, particularly the bloodthirsty eagerness of early British airmen for bombing Iraq, and of Winston Churchill's unbridled enthusiasm for using a weapon of mass destruction (poison gas) on the 'uncivilised tribes' of Iraq.

As a writer, I quickly found myself gripped and fascinated by the challenge of writing a sequence of plays for the same group of actors, all linked by theme and setting. Once the idea of a linked sequence had taken root, the project would not go away. Two plays eventually led to a third, and finally a fourth. The older archives of Broadmoor are now open to the public and can be seen at the Berkshire Records Office. They offered a wealth of material to help me in writing the plays. Part of what fascinated me about Broadmoor was that its very existence goes to the heart of the debate about murder and personal responsibility. Chester Minor, a man completely insane for much of his life, expressed deep remorse for the murder he committed. At the same time, British airmen and politicians, in the grip of a different kind of collective insanity, cheerfully bombed and gassed their way across a whole country without apology, murdering thousands in their pursuit of the British imperial project. This paradox was at the heart of the first two plays I wrote. A fascinating footnote to my exploration of this theme was that Broadmoor at that time operated a 'Gentleman's Wing' where better off and more educated patients enjoyed better conditions and could actually hire other patients to work for them.

Broadmoor is bound up with the development of ideas about madness and of psychiatry, some of which are explored in the plays. Many of the murderers sent to Broadmoor from the 19th century to the present day have a kind of notorious celebrity. However the four Broadmoor plays are all dedicated to the murder victims, and the lives of these victims is very much centre stage, two of them actually appearing as ghosts. The question of whether there is more to our fascination than mere prurience preoccupied me. Psychotic patients are often consciously engaged in a process of personal myth-making. In the course of writing these plays, I came to believe that, at a deeper level, our fascination with their often strange and gruesome crimes stems from the fact that, in an increasingly secular age, the crimes they have committed can sometimes assume a kind of mythic significance for all of us. The plays draw on Greek, Egyptian and Christian mythology to explore this idea. After all, these mythologies are all full of stories of astonishing violence and horror, often with deep psychotic resonances.

Of course, the lives of these Broadmoor patients and their crimes are also inherently theatrical. This was never more the case than with Richard Prince, an embittered, out-of-work actor who murdered matinee idol William Terriss at the stage door of the Adelphi Theatre in 1897. Prince later conducted the Broadmoor Orchestra for many years. *The Murder Club* imagines a fictitious encounter between him and Ronald True that dramatises the issue of personal and collective responsibility for murder set against the background of an entertainment the two men are organising at Broadmoor. The title of the Quartet, *Lullabies of Broadmoor* is itself a nod to the dark irony of these terrible crimes becoming the stuff of entertainment.

Theatre and performance were always a prominent feature of the regime at Broadmoor. It is hard to imagine now, but for many years, right up until the 1940s in fact, Broadmoor patients put on an Annual show, open to the public, which sold out every year. Richard Dadd, the famous Victorian painter actually redecorated the theatre at Broadmoor during his time there, although his work is now sadly lost. Dadd was the subject of *The Demon Box* which I wrote in 2007. He showed his first symptoms of insanity while abroad on the Grand Tour. While in Egypt, he believed he had been contacted by the god Osiris and received instructions to murder his father, which he duly did. *The Demon Box* imagines an encounter between Dadd and Chester Minor based on their shared love of painting and fascination with mythology.

I wrote *Venus at Broadmoor* in 2010. It dramatises the story of Christiana

Edmunds who went on a random poisoning spree in Brighton in 1870 before ending up in Broadmoor. Although the last to be written, it is actually the first play in the quartet, helping to set the scene for the other plays and setting out some of the themes that are to be explored again in subsequent plays.

The four plays of the quartet are bound together by John Coleman, the only character in all four plays, who is a Principal Attendant on the Gentleman's Block and interacts deeply with each of the patients. Coleman is the narrator in three of the plays, but is a very active participant in the action also. A flawed character himself, the struggles with his own demons give him a particular empathy with those in his charge. He is not particularly interested in the diagnosis inmates are given, but tries to cultivate relationships with them based on respect, honesty and a common, shared humanity. Like the public of his day, and many in the current day, he is broadly sceptical about the use of an insanity diagnosis to evade personal responsibility. This scepticism, and his curiosity to dig deeper into people's motivations is one of the driving forces of the plays which all try to explore the dark, complex mixture of life experiences that contribute to insanity and the crimes people sometimes commit under its influence.

The four plays all start from the premise that insanity is often an understandable response to intolerable pressures and traumatic life experiences such as sexual abuse or the experience of war, or sometimes, simply a desperate response to the absence of love. Personally, in my time working within mental health, I have always found this a much more useful way of understanding mental health problems than talk of chemical imbalances in the brain and genetic predispositions. The Broadmoor Quartet explores this idea in some depth as well as looking at how the apparently insane content of psychosis can often be made intelligible once we understand its roots in the real life experience of the person subject to those particular delusions.

The plays were all written so that they could be stand-alone pieces, but that seen together, they would take the audience on a deeper and richer journey. Each play is just over an hour long. Nine years after the first play was produced, all four plays are now to be produced together and toured in 2011. It's an exciting conclusion to a project that has preoccupied me for so long.

Chris Bianchi
Dr Orange / Richard Dadd / Ronald True / George Merrett
Theatre includes *King Lear*, *The Provok'd Wife*, *The Seagull* (The Peter Hall Company at The Old Vic), *The Nutcracker*, *Filumena* (Theatre Royal Bath), *Julius Caesar*, *Antony and Cleopatra* (Shakespeare at The Tobacco Factory), *A Christmas Carol, Alice Through the Looking Glass*, *Blue/Orange* (The Tobacco Factory), *Aesop's Fables* (Bristol Old Vic and International Tour), *No Loud Bangs* series, *The Rivals*, *The Owl Who Was Afraid of the Dark*, *Penetrator* and *Addicted to Love* (Bristol Old Vic), *The Hunchback of Notre Dame, Charlotte's Web* (Duke's Playhouse, Lancaster), *Ministry of Fear*, *A Flying Visit*, *The Crowstarver*, *Bonjour Bob* (Theatre Alibi National Tours) and *Clown* (Travelling Light).

Chris Courtenay
Dr. Beard / William Chester Minor / Richard Prince
At the Finborough Theatre, Chris appeared in *Wilderness* and *The Murder Club* (2004) and *The New Morality* (2005).
Theatre includes *A Christmas Carol* (Trafalgar Studios), *Henry VIII* (Shakespeare's Globe), *The Master and Margarita*, *Akhmatova's Salted Herring* (Menier Chocolate Factory), *Romeo and Juliet* (Jermyn Street Theatre), *The Dybbuk* (King's Head Theatre), *Fallen Angels* (Vienna's English Theatre), *Julius Caesar* (Leptis Magna), *The Blue Room* (Tabard Theatre), *Rumplestiltskin and Other Grizzly Tales* (Wimbledon Studio Theatre), *Macbeth*, *Hamlet* (Cambridge Shakespeare Festival) and *The Public Eye* (Etcetera Theatre).
Television, Film and Radio includes *The Chilcot Enquiry'*, *Royal Wealth*, *Alice and Camilla*, *Credo*, *Déjà Vu*, *The Furred Man*, *The Bed Guy* and Thor Heyerdahl in BBC Radio 4's *A Thor in One's Side*.

Chris Donnelly
John Coleman
Theatre includes *A Midsummer Night's Dream*, *The Tempest*, *Othello*, *The Winter's Tale*, *A Midsummer Night's Dream*, *Measure For Measure*, *The Taming of the Shrew*, *Troilus and Cressida* (Shakespeare at The Tobacco Factory), *The Winter's Tale* (Southwark Playhouse), *Twelfth Night* and *Macbeth* (US Tours), *Bent* (Courtyard Theatre), *Edge of Darkness* (National Tour) and *One Flea Spare* (Old Red Lion Theatre).
Television includes *Four Seasons*, *Vital Signs*, *Fat Friends*, *Silent Witness*, *Wire in the Blood*, *EastEnders*, *Drop the Dead Donkey*, *Casualty*, *Reckless*, *Wycliffe* and *The Verdict*.
Radio includes *Soldier Soldier*, *Call Waiting* and *Gilgamesh* – all award-winning plays for BBC Radio 4.

Violet Ryder
Christiana Edmunds / Ariel / Olive Young / Eliza Merrett
Theatre includes the critically acclaimed *Brief Encounter* (Kneehigh), *Pride and Prejudice* (Theatre Royal Bath and National Tour), *Venus at Broadmoor* (Alma Tavern, Bristol), *The Walker Tribe*, *A Case of Deception* (The London Quest Company), *Richard III*, *Love's Labour's Lost* (Cambridge Shakespeare Festival) and *From Lamplight to Limelight* and *The Passing Preciousness of Dreams* (Canterbury Festival).

Steve Hennessy Playwright

At the Finborough Theatre, Steve was Playwright-in-Residence from 2004 to 2007, and has had three plays produced at the venue including *Wilderness* and *The Murder Club* (2004) and *The Demon Box* as part of *Vibrant – An Anniversary Festival of Finborough Playwrights* (2010).

Steve has had twenty two plays staged in Bristol, London, Manchester and elsewhere, and four radio plays broadcast in Britain, Ireland and Germany. Steve founded and runs Stepping Out Theatre, the country's leading mental health theatre group, working with mental health service users and producing work exploring mental health themes. His play *Still Life* won the Venue magazine 'Best New Play' award in 2001 and *Moonshadow* was a *Time Out* Critics' Choice Show of the Week in 2009.

Chris Loveless Director

At the Finborough Theatre, Chris directed *The Demon Box* as part of *Vibrant – An Anniversary Festival of Finborough Playwrights* (2010).

Trained at the Bristol Old Vic Theatre School. He is Artistic Director of Fallen Angel Theatre Company and an Associate Director of both the White Bear Theatre and Stepping Out Theatre. Directing includes *The Remains of the Day*, named *Evening Standard* Critics' Choice (Union Theatre), *Normal* (The Tobacco Factory), *Moonshadow*, named Critics' Choice and Show of the Week in *Time Out*, *Dracula* and *The Custom of the Country*, named *Time Out* Critics' Choice (White Bear Theatre), *Venus at Broadmoor*, *Vampire Nights*, *Ray Collins Dies On Stage*, *Walter's Monkey* and *Thursday Coma* (Alma Tavern, Bristol), *Stairway to Heaven*, for which he was nominated for an OffWestEnd Award for Best Director (Blue Elephant Theatre), *Blavatsky's Tower* (Brockley Jack Studio Theatre), *The 24 Hour Plays* (Ustinov Theatre). www.chrisloveless.com

Ann Stiddard Designer
At the Finborough Theatre, Ann designed *Wilderness* and *The Murder Club* (2004) and *Viral Sutra* (2006).
Ann is a joint Artistic Director of Theatre West who have been a leading company for new writing in the South West for the last twenty years. She has designed dozens of productions for them at the Alma Tavern, Bristol. Other work includes *The Two Noble Kinsmen*, *Shang-a-Lang*, *Blue Heart*, *Far Away* (Bristol Old Vic), *Little Pictures* (Bristol Old Vic and Tour of Latvia), *Six Beckett Pieces* (Tour of Latvia), *A Doll's House* (QEH, Bristol) and many productions for the Edinburgh Festival. She has designed all of Stepping Out's productions for the last ten years.

Tim Bartlett Lighting Designer
At the Finborough Theatre, Tim designed the lighting for *Wilderness* and *The Murder Club* (2004).
Tim has designed lighting for dozens of productions for Theatre West, Stepping Out Theatre and other Bristol companies. His work includes *Ray Collins Dies On Stage*, *The Vagina Monologues* (Alma Tavern, Bristol) and *Seven Go Mad in Thebes!* (QEH, Bristol).

Rebecca Sellors Costume Designer
Rebecca has worked for over six years in the industry, designing and making costumes for television, film and theatre including several years at Angels Costumiers. Her work includes *Bond Girls*, *Play Time*, *Venus at Broadmoor* (Alma Tavern, Bristol), *Chicago* (DET NY Theatre), *The Airmen and the Headhunters* (Icon Film) and *In This Style* (Hollow Tree Pictures).

Stepping Out Theatre Producer

Founded in 1997, and with 35 productions to its credit, Stepping Out Theatre is the country's leading mental health theatre group. It has produced a wide range of work on mental health themes and is open to people who have used mental health services and their supporters. It offers mental health service users the opportunity to work alongside people with professional experience of writing, directing and acting, some of whom are service users themselves. The group has won two national awards in recognition of its high quality and groundbreaking work in mental health. www.steppingouttheatre.co.uk

Simon James Collier Producer

Simon is the CEO and Co Founder of the award-winning Okai Collier Company. He has produced and been the Creative Director on over sixty plays and musicals including *1888*, *The Remains of the Day* (Union Theatre), *Animate!* (Prince of Wales Theatre), *Bloodline*, *Project Snowflake*, *Blavatsky's Tower* (Jack Studio Theatre), *Collision*, *A Mother Speaks*, *The Smilin' State*, *A Wrongful Execution* (Hackney Empire), *Purlie*, *Passion*, *Elegies*, *A... My Name Is Alice* (Bridewell), *Great Balls Of Fire* (Cambridge Theatre), *Preacherosity*, *My Matisse*, *The Dorchester* (Jermyn Street Theatre), *Shiny Happy People* with Victoria Wood (Queen's Theatre, Hornchurch), *Whole Lotta Shakin'* (Belgrade Theatre, Coventry), *La Vie en rose* (King's Head Theatre and Towngate Theatre, Basildon), *Normal* (The Tobacco Factory), *Hedwig and The Angry Inch* (K52 Theatre, Frankfurt), *Ruthless* (Stratford Circus) and *Dracula, Gifted* (White Bear Theatre). Simon recently produced *Dance With Me*, his first feature film, and has written a series of books for young adults. He has also been the Executive Director of London's Bridewell Theatre and Artistic Consultant to Jermyn Street Theatre.

FINBOROUGH | THEATRE

Fringe Theatre of the Year 2010

STAGE 100 AWARDS

Winner – *London Theatre Reviews'* Empty Space Peter Brook Award 2010
"One of the most stimulating venues in London, fielding a programme that is a bold mix of trenchant, politically thought-provoking new drama and shrewdly chosen revivals of neglected works from the past." *The Independent*

"A disproportionately valuable component of the London theatre ecology. Its programme combines new writing and revivals, in selections intelligent and audacious." *Financial Times*

"A blazing beacon of intelligent endeavour, nurturing new writers while finding and reviving neglected curiosities from home and abroad."
The Daily Telegraph

Founded in 1980, the multi-award-winning Finborough Theatre presents plays and music theatre, concentrated exclusively on new writing and rediscoveries from the 19th and 20th centuries. We offer a stimulating and inclusive programme, appealing to theatregoers of all generations and from a broad spectrum of the population. Behind the scenes, we continue to discover and develop a new generation of theatre makers – through our vibrant Literary Department, our internship programme, our Resident Assistant Director Programme, and our partnership with the National Theatre Studio – the Leverhulme Bursary for Emerging Directors.

Despite remaining completely unfunded, the Finborough Theatre has an unparalleled track record of attracting the finest creative talent to work with us, as well as discovering new playwrights who go on to become leading voices in British theatre. Under Artistic Director Neil McPherson, it has discovered some of the UK's most exciting new playwrights including Laura Wade, James Graham, Mike Bartlett, Sarah Grochala, Jack Thorne, Simon Vinnicombe, Alexandra Wood, Al Smith, Nicholas de Jongh and Anders Lustgarten.

Artists working at the theatre in the 1980s included Clive Barker, Rory Bremner, Nica Burns, Kathy Burke, Ken Campbell, Jane Horrocks and Claire Dowie. In the 1990s, the Finborough Theatre became known for new writing including Naomi Wallace's first play *The War Boys*; Rachel Weisz in David Farr's *Neville Southall's Washbag*; four plays by Anthony Neilson including *Penetrator* and *The Censor*, both of which transferred to the Royal Court Theatre; and new plays by Tony Marchant, David Eldridge, Mark Ravenhill and Phil Willmott. New writing development included a number of works that went to become modern classics including Mark Ravenhill's *Shopping and F***king*, Conor McPherson's *This Lime Tree Bower*, Naomi Wallace's *Slaughter City* and Martin McDonagh's *The Pillowman*.

Since 2000, new British plays have included Laura Wade's London debut with her adaptation of W.H. Davies' *Young Emma*, commissioned for the Finborough Theatre; James Graham's *Albert's Boy* with Victor Spinetti; Sarah Grochala's *S27*; Peter Nichols' *Lingua Franca*, which transferred Off-Broadway; Joy Wilkinson's *Fair*; Nicholas de Jongh's *Plague Over England*; and Jack Thorne's *Fanny and Faggot*, all of which transferred to the West End. Many of the Finborough Theatre's new plays have been published and are on sale from our website.

UK premieres of foreign plays have included Brad Fraser's *Wolfboy*; Lanford Wilson's *Sympathetic Magic*; Larry Kramer's *The Destiny of Me*; Tennessee Williams' *Something Cloudy, Something Clear*; the English premiere of Robert McLellan's Scots language classic, *Jamie the Saxt*; and three West End transfers – Frank McGuinness' *Gates of Gold* with William Gaunt and John Bennett, Joe DiPietro's *F***ing Men* and Craig Higginson's *Dream of the Dog* with Janet Suzman.

Rediscoveries of neglected work have included the first London revivals of Rolf Hochhuth's *Soldiers* and *The Representative*; both parts of Keith Dewhurst's *Lark Rise to Candleford*; *The Women's War*, an evening of original suffragette plays; *Etta Jenks* with Clarke Peters and Daniela Nardini; Noël Coward's first play, *The Rat Trap*; Charles Wood's *Jingo* with Susannah Harker; two sell-out productions by J.M. Barrie – *What Every Woman Knows* and *Quality Street*; and Emlyn Williams' *Accolade* with Aden Gillett, Graham Seed and Saskia Wickham.

Music Theatre has included the new (premieres from Grant Olding, Charles Miller, Michael John LaChuisa, Adam Guettel,

Andrew Lippa and Adam Gwon – *Ordinary Days* which transferred to the West End) and the old (the UK premiere of Rodgers and Hammerstein's *State Fair* which also transferred to the West End, and the acclaimed *Celebrating British Music Theatre* series, reviving forgotten British musicals).

The Finborough Theatre won *London Theatre Reviews'* Empty Space Peter Brook Award in 2010, the Empty Space Peter Brook Mark Marvin Award in 2004, the Empty Space Peter Brook Award's Dan Crawford Pub Theatre Award in 2005 and 2008 and awards for Best Director and Best Lighting Designer in the 2011 Off West End Awards. It is the only theatre without public funding to be awarded the Pearson Playwriting Award bursary for writers Chris Lee in 2000, Laura Wade in 2005 (who also went on to win the Critics' Circle Theatre Award for Most Promising Playwright, the George Devine Award and an Olivier Award nomination), for James Graham in 2006, for Al Smith in 2007, for Anders Lustgarten in 2009 and Simon Vinnicombe in 2010. Three bursary holders (Laura Wade, James Graham and Anders Lustgarten) have also won the Catherine Johnson Award for Best Play written by a bursary holder. Artistic Director Neil McPherson won the *Fringe Report* Best Artistic Director award in 2009, The Writers' Guild Award for the Encouragement of New Writing in 2010 and Best Artistic Director at the 2011 Off West End Awards.

www.finboroughtheatre.co.uk

FINBOROUGH | THEATRE

118 Finborough Road, London SW10 9ED
admin@finboroughtheatre.co.uk
www.finboroughtheatre.co.uk

Supported by
The Leverhulme Bursary for Emerging Directors is a partnership between the National Theatre Studio and the Finborough Theatre, supported by The Leverhulme Trust.

The Finborough Theatre is a member of the Independent Theatre Council, Musical Theatre Matters UK (MTM:UK) and The Earl's Court Society www.earlscourtsociety.org.uk

Ecovenue is a European Regional Development Fund backed three-year initiative of The Theatres Trust, aiming to improve the environmental sustainability of 48 small to medium-sized performing arts spaces across London. www.ecovenue.org.uk

The Finborough Wine Café
Contact Rob Malcolm or Monique Ziervogel on 020 7373 0745 or finboroughwinecafe@gmail.com

Online
Join us at Facebook, Twitter, MySpace and YouTube.

Mailing
Email admin@finboroughtheatre.co.uk or give your details to our Box Office staff to join our free email list. If you would like to be sent a free season leaflet every three months, just include your postal address and postcode.

Feedback

We welcome your comments, complaints and suggestions. Write to Finborough Theatre, 118 Finborough Road, London SW10 9ED or email us at admin@finboroughtheatre.co.uk

Friends

The Finborough Theatre is a registered charity. We receive no public funding, and rely solely on the support of our audiences. Please do consider supporting us by becoming a member of our Friends of the Finborough Theatre scheme. There are four categories of Friends, each offering a wide range of benefits.

Richard Tauber Friends – Harry MacAuslan. Brian Smith.

Lionel Monckton Friends – Bridget MacDougall.

William Terriss Friends – Philip Hooker. Leo and Janet Liebster. Peter Lobl. Bhagat Sharma. Thurloe and Lyndhurst LLP.

Smoking is not permitted in the auditorium and the use of cameras and recording equipment is strictly prohibited.

In accordance with the requirements of the Royal Borough of Kensington and Chelsea:

1. The public may leave at the end of the performance by all doors and such doors must at that time be kept open.

2. All gangways, corridors, staircases and external passageways intended for exit shall be left entirely free from obstruction whether permanent or temporary.

3. Persons shall not be permitted to stand or sit in any of the gangways intercepting the seating or to sit in any of the other gangways.

The Finborough Theatre is licensed by the Royal Borough of Kensington and Chelsea to The Steam Industry, a registered charity and a company limited by guarantee. Registered in England no. 3448268. Registered Charity no. 1071304. Registered Office: 118 Finborough Road, London SW10 9ED. The Steam Industry is under the Artistic Direction of Phil Willmott. www.philwillmott.co.uk

Air Conditioning and Heating Appeal

We are currently fundraising for the cost of the newly installed air conditioning and heating for the auditorium. We are a completely unfunded registered charity. If you would like to make a donation towards the installation of air conditioning, do please speak to the Box Office Staff.

Steve Hennessy

LULLABIES OF BROADMOOR
A BROADMOOR QUARTET

OBERON BOOKS
LONDON

WWW.OBERONBOOKS.COM

First published in 2011 by Oberon Books Ltd
521 Caledonian Road, London N7 9RH
Tel: +44 (0) 20 7607 3637 / Fax: +44 (0) 20 7607 3629
e-mail: info@oberonbooks.com
www.oberonbooks.com

A catalogue record for this book is available from the British Library.

ISBN: 978-1-84943-162-0

Cover photography by Jose Navarro

Printed in Great Britain by CPI Antony Rowe, Chippenham.

Contents

VENUS AT BROADMOOR

'Venus at Broadmoor' is dedicated to Sidney Barker
(1867 – 1871)

Characters

CHRISTIANA EDMUNDS (1829–1907)
Broadmoor patient 1872 till her death.
Found guilty of string of poisonings in 1870–71,
including one murder.

JOHN COLEMAN
Principal attendant, Block 2, Broadmoor

DR. WILLIAM ORANGE
Medical Superintendent, Broadmoor, 1870–86

DR. CHARLES BEARD
Married lover of Christiana

SET

One section of the stage is Dr. Orange's Broadmoor office with a writing bureau, two chairs and perhaps some set dressing. The other area is a neutral space where all other scenes take place. There is a small low bed to one side of this area which is lit only for the scene in which this area becomes the Infirmary. At other times, this is a meeting room space without furniture where the Social Committee meets, or it is a composite of the Royal Albion Hotel and other places where the flashback scenes in Brighton take place. One offstage position needed for exits and Christiana's costume changes.

(Stage dark. Music – 'Venus' from Holst's 'Planets Suite'. DR. ORANGE working at his desk, CHRISTIANA adjusting her make up. DR. BEARD strolling along beach with straw hat and cane. Low light up on COLEMAN.)

COLEMAN: Is there a cure for fallin' in love? The madness of it! Sharpening all your senses and makin' you feel so alive, you just can't stop smiling, all wide-eyed with wonder like a kid in a sweetshop. Close your eyes and you're lost! Like smellin' a full-blown rose in a garden on a warm summer evenin'. Or bitin' into a soft chocolate cream so sweet it brings a tear to your eye.

(He bites into a chocolate cream. Closes eyes.)

That was me in the summer of 1872. I was tryin' to lay off the drink at the time, as you do, so I 'ad my sweet tooth back, an' the craving for my old favourites. Oh, you little temptation! Come to daddy!

(Finishes off the sweet.)

Amazing! I wasn't too old, or too cynical after all. An' it didn't matter that I barely knew 'er, or that she probably didn't feel the same. That just made it more like my first time all over again, and it felt like it would last … forever.

(Music fades. Lights up.)

These never tasted quite the same after 1872. The penny dreadfuls were screaming …

CHRISTIANA: Beware the Chocolate Cream Poisoner!

COLEMAN: Christiana Edmunds probably didn't like the title, but what else were they gonna call 'er? She was …

(All go into melodramatic penny dreadful routine.)

CHRISTIANA: A woman! Who fell madly in love …

COLEMAN: With a doctor …

DR. BEARD: Dr. Charles Beard.

COLEMAN: A *married* doctor.

CHRISTIANA: The madness of love! Our passionate letters!

COLEMAN: *(Shakes head.)* Dr. Beard! Really!

DR. BEARD: I don't know what possessed me with those letters! But nothing happened!

CHRISTIANA: Well he would say that, wouldn't he?

COLEMAN: What about the wife?

CHRISTIANA: Emily Beard had … let herself go.

COLEMAN: In what way?

CHRISTIANA: *Chocolate creams*!

(All three gasp with horror.)

DR. BEARD: *(Laughs.)* Well, if I ever wanted to get my wife out of the way, it wouldn't be difficult to work out where to put the strychnine! *(Beat.)* Joking, Chrissie!

COLEMAN: After a year or so, Chrissie delivered a present to fat Emily.

CHRISTIANA: Mrs. Beard, I won't take no for an answer! I know they are your favourite, and what does it matter that Charles disapproves of you eating quite so many! I took the liberty of calling while he's out and he need never know. We ladies are entitled to some secrets, are we not? I do so hope you'll enjoy them!

(DR. BEARD rounds on her.)

DR. BEARD: Emily was violently ill after eating some of the chocolates you gave her. In God's name, what were you thinking of?

CHRISTIANA: Are you insane, Charles? How could you believe I was capable of such a thing! I bought the same chocolates for myself from Maynards and have spent the whole weekend ill in bed. I was affected far worse than Emily!

COLEMAN: Of course 'e didn't believe 'er.

DR. BEARD: Of course I believe you Christiana. But all this must now stop.

CHRISTIANA: *(Whispers.)* How can it stop?

DR. BEARD: My nerves cannot take any more!

CHRISTIANA: You're a doctor! Cure your nerves!

DR. BEARD: If Emily ever found out …

COLEMAN: I thought nothing happened, Dr. Beard?

DR. BEARD: Nothing did happen.

(CHRISTIANA advances in a rage holding up letters.)

CHRISTIANA: The things you wrote? The things we did? Nothing!? This?

DR. BEARD: My beautiful one … my goddess!

CHRISTIANA: This?

DR. BEARD: Our love is a revelation. Like nothing I've ever known.

CHRISTIANA: Forever, you said!

DR. BEARD: That was last year!

CHRISTIANA: Sweetness almost beyond endurance, you said.

DR. BEARD: It was poisoning us!

(Pause.)

I cannot see you again. We must return to our separate lives.

COLEMAN: There'd been too many close shaves for Dr. Beard. 'E bottled out.

DR. BEARD: But the poisoning was only just beginning. An epidemic all over Brighton! Violent illness usually following the consumption of confectionery. Bags of unopened sweets left temptingly in public places.

COLEMAN: Other sweets purchased, poisoned and then returned to Maynards the confectioners to catch victims at random.

DR. BEARD: Six prominent local women also received anonymous parcels of poisoned sweets, including, once again …

CHRISTIANA: Emily Beard.

COLEMAN: But the poisoner's bloody useless! Doesn't manage to kill a single person!

DR. BEARD: Until 12th June 1871. And then, it isn't Emily.

(Loud FX of crashing waves.)

Mr. Charlie Miller, out for a day at the seaside in Brighton, takes his four-year-old nephew Sidney Barker to Maynards sweetshop. *(As Uncle Charlie.)* What'll it be then little Sidney?

COLEMAN: *(As SIDNEY.)* I can't make up my mind, uncle Charlie!

DR. BEARD: *(As Uncle Charlie.)* Come on, lad! You'll have to go soon! Your mum and dad are waiting! We've got a train to catch!

COLEMAN: *(As SIDNEY.)* All right! *(Beat.)* What are those?

DR. BEARD: *(As Uncle Charlie.)* Chocolate creams?

CHRISTIANA: He knows they're expensive. Not like the cheap confectionery he's used to …

DR. BEARD: Boiled sweets …

CHRISTIANA: Sherberts …

DR. BEARD: Licorice …

CHRISTIANA: Special! A whole new world of sweetness and pleasure.

COLEMAN: *(As Sidney.)* Chocolate creams please, Uncle Charlie!

CHRISTIANA: On the way back to the train station a pretty lady with a parasol smiles at him and he smiles back.

DR. BEARD: He counts up all the good things in the day.

COLEMAN: The train journey.

DR. BEARD: The donkey ride on the beach.

COLEMAN: Makin' the sandcastles.

DR. BEARD: Paddling in a warm sea.

CHRISTIANA: Running all the way to the end of Chain Pier, through the seaspray of the big waves.

DR. BEARD: He smiles up at Uncle Charlie, pops a chocolate cream into his mouth and feels it flood with an unfamiliar sweetness.

CHRISTIANA: He'll have to go soon, but he knows he'll remember this moment forever. A perfect end to a perfect day.

COLEMAN: Sunshine …

DR. BEARD: The endless sea …

COLEMAN: The waves crashin' onto the sand …

CHRISTIANA: And blue sky stretching into the distance …

DR. BEARD: Forever.

(Pause. FX of waves stops abruptly.)

With mounting horror, I realised that Christiana must be the poisoner. I went to the Police. On the seventh of

September 1871, she was charged with the attempted murder of my wife Emily and the murder of Sidney Barker.

(Lighting change. Mood change.)

COLEMAN: Dr. Beard was the first of a large herd of doctors who tramped through the Chocolate Cream Poisoner's life in 1872. Five of 'em assessed 'er mental state before and after trial. All regular expert witnesses in insanity cases. Dr. William Wood, formerly of Bedlam, now runnin' a private asylum.

DR. BEARD: *(As Dr. Wood.)* She satisfies the principal MacNaughton rule. She cannot distinguish right from wrong and is clearly insane.

COLEMAN: Doctor Charles Lockhart Robertson. Superintendent of the Sussex County Asylum.

DR. BEARD: *(As Dr. Robertson.)* I believe she belongs to the morally defective group of lunatics.

COLEMAN: The old prophet of doom, Henry Maudsley, Editor of the British Mental Journal.

DR. BEARD: *(As Dr. Maudsley.)* In physical organization, the convict presents those marks of low and feeble cerebral development which characterises this class of criminals.

COLEMAN: Sir William Gull, personal physician to Prince Albert.

DR. BEARD: *(As Sir William Gull.)* These acts were the fruit of a weak and disordered intellect with confused and perverted feelings of a most marked insane character!

COLEMAN: And finally the Broadmoor Medical Superintendent 'imself, our very own Dr. William Orange.

DR. ORANGE: The crime of murder she seems incapable of realising as having been committed by her, though she fully admits the purchasing and distributing the poisons as set forth in the several counts against her.

COLEMAN: It was settled then.

(DR. BEARD exits. DR. ORANGE goes to his office. Picks up a letter.)

DR. ORANGE: Confirmation, Mr. Coleman. The Home Secretary has commuted her death sentence to detention in Broadmoor at Her Majesty's pleasure. Inform Matron to have a room made ready on the women's wing.

COLEMAN: Is there a cure for madness? Dr. Orange believed passionately that there was, and that the asylum was the place to do it. Ran a big County asylum for ten years and deputy in charge of Broadmoor for the first seven years of its existence before being recently promoted to Medical Superintendent. Unmarried, no kids. Progress towards the final cure was 'is life's obsession. In fact, 'e was working on a big speech on that very topic for the Annual Meeting of the Medico-Psychological Association. I used to 'ear 'im practisin' when I went by 'is office.

(DR. ORANGE rehearses speech in office with his notes.)

DR. ORANGE: Remember! Not so long ago, in Hospitals and private madhouses across the land, men and women were routinely chained to the walls and floors, and left lying amid their own filth. Then at Hanwell Asylum, the great reforming Superintendent John Connolly started a revolution! Nineteen tons of those shameful shackles torn from his building alone! The torch he lit burns bright to this day, even at Broadmoor. Imagine! We house individuals whose insanity takes the most violent forms, and yet there has not been a single use of mechanical restraint in the first eight years of Broadmoor's operation! And since the Parliamentary Commission, the whole country now has a new generation of County Asylums which are regularly inspected, licensed, and accountable. Driving this progress has been our shared determination to create the humane and moral regime which is at the heart of the modern asylum. I confidently predict that this regime will lead to an ever-increasing number of lunatics cured and returned to society.

COLEMAN: At Broadmoor, 'cure' means firstly understanding and taking responsibility for your crime. So when Christiana arrived on the 5th of July 1872, denying any responsibility for murdering a child, I assumed the Doctor would want the work with 'er to start fairly sharpish. But 'e 'ad two reasons for delaying the introductory meeting.

(Lights up on DR. ORANGE in his office.)

DR. ORANGE: The focus of Miss Edmunds' crime was a relationship with a doctor. She flirted outrageously with the three doctors who testified her insanity at trial, and with Dr. Gull and I when we assessed her in prison on behalf of the Home Office.

COLEMAN: Medical nymphomania!

DR. ORANGE: Quite. Also, the view of all five of us was that this woman is currently incapable of understanding her crime. I would rather wait for some sign of change in her before expending more energy on the case.

COLEMAN: I understand sir. *(To audience.)* Made sense to concentrate effort when and where a cure was more likely. Cure rates weren't high, an' I'd seen the doctor gettin' very worn down by the work over recent years. Cure was the last thing on Christiana's mind. As soon as she found out I was Secretary of the Social Committee, she requested a meeting with me, and there was only one thing she was interested in.

CHRISTIANA: The ball!

COLEMAN: An' that's 'ow it all began.

(CHRISTIANA walks briskly up to COLEMAN.)

CHRISTIANA: Mr. Coleman, let us dance!

COLEMAN: *(Stunned.)* Miss?

CHRISTIANA: Let us fly across that floor together, aware of nothing but the thrilling crescendos of the music, and the excited beating of our hearts! Just say the word Mr. Coleman! I will dance with you all night, or until we both drop from exhaustion. Assuming of course that you want to dance with me? And you don't have two left feet? You are Mr. John Coleman aren't you? Who runs the social committee?

(CHRISTIANA freezes. 'Venus' music.)

COLEMAN: *(To audience.)* I was lost. It was like that. *(Snaps his fingers.)* Love? Infatuation? It didn't matter. Nothing was going to happen. But something had happened! And by the end of the meetin' I was shaking. Like a man desperate for a drink. Which is what I was. How could anyone 'ave that effect on me at my age? Let alone someone who'd done what she 'ad. But where everyone else saw the Chocolate Cream Poisoner, I suddenly saw this funny, clever … intoxicating woman. Tried to salvage some pride, tellin' myself she'd 'ave no idea of 'er effect on me. But she saw the moon-eyed stare and the big, stupid smile. She probably already knew she could ask me to do anything, and I was ready to make a complete fool of myself.

(Music ceases. CHRISTIANA unfreezes and claps a hand over her mouth.)

CHRISTIANA: Oh no! I've made a complete fool of myself! You're not Mr. Coleman at all?

COLEMAN: No. *(Beat.)* Yes! Course I am! Miss Edmunds, I presume?

(She holds out her hand and shakes his.)

CHRISTIANA: Please call me Christiana.

COLEMAN: Can't really do that Miss. Regulations.

CHRISTIANA: Oh John, what a pity!

COLEMAN: And it has to be 'Mr. Coleman' I'm afraid.

CHRISTIANA: Oh, sorry John! Never mind. Well, I've been told you run the Social Committee.

COLEMAN: Correct!

CHRISTIANA: And there's to be a ball?

COLEMAN: Regular event!

CHRISTIANA: I could quibble about that use of 'regular'.

COLEMAN: As clockwork! Every November.

CHRISTIANA: Oohhhhh! *(Laughs, stamps foot.)* Why so seldom?

COLEMAN: Doctors aren't keen on dancing, Miss. They say it gets inmates … over-excited.

CHRISTIANA: Heavens forfend! Dr. Orange doesn't dance then?

COLEMAN: I don't think wild 'orses could drag the doctor onto a dance floor.

CHRISTIANA: *(Whinnies.)* Perhaps I can be the first to try!

COLEMAN: 'E's away in London that weekend Miss. Big meeting for the 'Eads of Asylums.

CHRISTIANA: No coincidence I'm sure, but what a pity! You know he assessed me personally for the Home Office?

COLEMAN: 'E did mention it.

CHRISTIANA: I remember thinking then he was a cold fish. But his assessment did prevent me from being hanged by the neck until I was dead, so I'm not complaining! When will I have my appointment to see him and say thank you?

COLEMAN: You're … on the list, Miss.

CHRISTIANA: I assume you dance?

COLEMAN: What I lack in co-ordination, I try to make up for with enthusiasm.

CHRISTIANA: I shall save the first and last dance on my card for you!

COLEMAN: Then Cinders, you shall definitely go to the ball!

CHRISTIANA: I've loved dancing since I was a child. Little dancing princess, father called me. Funnily enough, he ended up in an asylum. He used to say my mother had driven him there. 'How did she do that?' people would ask, and he'd reply gaily 'In a Hackney carriage!'

COLEMAN: 'Ackney carriage! Tha's good!

CHRISTIANA: Dancing is the only time I'm ever truly happy. I forget everything else. But Mr. Coleman, I'm going to need your help! I need new clothes and make up for the ball.

COLEMAN: Not really my department, Miss. Talk to Matron.

CHRISTIANA: Oh, already tried! But however patiently I explain, she just keeps repeating 'Regulations … what inmates are permitted … blah, blah.' It's very wearing, John. Honestly, it gives me a headache.

COLEMAN: I wish I could do more.

CHRISTIANA: Good! You can! My sister can supply all the clothes and make up I want. I just need to make arrangements for their … discreet delivery.

(CHRISTIANA freezes again. 'Venus' music. COLEMAN walks around her.)

COLEMAN: It's a disciplinary offence to smuggle anything into Broadmoor, but I was so … besotted, I took the risk. Christiana got 'er clothes an' make up. She'd smile whenever she saw me after that, an' be eager to chat. Just as I'd hoped. I made excuses to be over in the women's blocks, tryin' to bump into 'er, without being too obvious. One day I suggested, ever so casually, that she join the Social Committee. An excuse to talk to 'er regularly. I know! *(Shakes head.)* I barely knew this woman! Harmless infatuation I told myself, except, on a day when I couldn't see 'er, it felt like my guts were being torn out. Tryin' to stay off the drink got even more difficult.

(He makes to put a chocolate cream in his mouth. CHRISTIANA unfreezes briefly and looks at him. He takes the sweet away from his mouth. Music stops.)

But when I tried to distract myself with chocolate creams now, I kept thinking of that four-year-old kid, and it made the pain in my guts even worse. There was only one way I could feel better about my obsession. She 'ad to be cured! I convinced myself that's what was gonna happen. Maybe I could even 'elp. And I was so 'appy she was in my life that within a few weeks, this … insane situation became normal. It became insane again when Dr. Orange read me Matron's first report on the new inmate.

(Doctor's office, him at desk reading from a paper.)

DR. ORANGE: But here's the truly interesting section. 'I then overheard Miss Edmunds say to another inmate, Miss Johnson, that she was "born out of the sea as *Venus* at Brighton." Miss Johnson asked "When was that, dear?" and Edmunds laughed and replied "September the fourth, 1870." When I quizzed her about this later, Edmunds denied saying anything of the kind and made derogatory remarks about my age, my hearing and my clothes.'

(Pause as he notices COLEMAN's discomfort.)

Mr. Coleman?

COLEMAN: *Venus*, sir!?

DR. ORANGE: The goddess of Love.

COLEMAN: I'm familiar with 'er *job* sir.

DR. ORANGE: That's what Matron overheard. Are you all right, Mr. Coleman?

COLEMAN: *(Beat.)* Of course sir. Venus! Pleasant change from Queen Victoria and the Virgin Mary!

DR. ORANGE: Perhaps more than that. This may be the *sign* we were waiting for! The birth of Venus Mr. Coleman! Uranus, the Sky God is copulating with Gaia, the Earth goddess, when he is attacked by his son Kronos who lops off his father's genitals with a sickle and throws them into the sea. They're swept away by the waves, and after a while a white foam spreads around them and Venus is born out of that. Uranus bleeds to death of his wound.

COLEMAN: Family life, eh sir?

DR. ORANGE: A tale of interest to our new inmate it seems.

COLEMAN: Sex and murder! No wonder Venus washed up at Broadmoor!

DR. ORANGE: I think she's already our household goddess, Mr. Coleman! Causing most of the despair, madness and murders that filled these walls.

COLEMAN: You're destroying all my romantic illusions, Doctor Orange!

DR. ORANGE: As I recall, the myths says she was vain and vicious, full of jealous rages and cruel punishments and constantly demanding sacrifices

COLEMAN: What about that date, sir?

DR. ORANGE: I checked. It's exactly a month before her first attempt to poison Mrs. Beard. This must be relevant.

COLEMAN: I imagine you'll be wanting that introductory meeting now?

DR. ORANGE: The time has come for our real work to begin. I smell the possibility of progress! And the cure of the Chocolate Cream Poisoner would be an impressive climax for my speech to the Association! God knows I'll need something. They've scheduled me to speak before Henry *Maudsley*, our wild-eyed prophet of doom! Tell Venus I'll see her in the morning at a time to suit her convenience.

(COLEMAN exits office. DR. ORANGE gets a paper out of his desk, skims over it and prepares to speak.)

COLEMAN: *(To audience.)* I knew she wasn't *really* Venus, but it shook me up! An insane explanation for my insane obsession! I was excited that at last we were getting started on 'er *cure*. I desperately wanted 'er to be well and 'appy. No particular reason. Don't look at me like that! I knew that she first 'ad to take responsibility for what she'd done. If anyone could make 'er do that, it was the doctor.

(DR. ORANGE speaks as if addressing an audience.)

DR. ORANGE: What is the humane and moral regime? It is based on the belief that kindness and compassion are the best tools for bringing the lunatic back to reason. Gentlemen, we should not blush to use the word, the new regime is based on love. It is the absence of love that creates the despair so many of our inmates feel. And for some, their first experience of any kind of love at all, may well be upon their admission to one of our institutions. This places on us a heavy and sacred trust. My fellow Medical Officers and Superintendents, the lunatic will not be cured without love.

(Lighting change. CHRISTIANA enters office.)

DR. ORANGE: Miss Edmunds, it's a pleasure to finally meet up again.

CHRISTIANA: A dubious pleasure surely doctor, given how long you've managed to resist it!

DR. ORANGE: If there were any emergency with your case, I would have made myself immediately available.

CHRISTIANA: I'm reassured! My small concerns do not constitute an emergency, but I'm glad of this opportunity to finally raise them with you.

DR. ORANGE: Before you do, Miss Edmunds, I should say that all my meetings with you, and indeed, all of the therapeutic regime here at Broadmoor have but one objective. This is the cure of that condition which brought you to commit your crimes. No cure is possible until you come to an understanding of what you have done, and can take some responsibility for it. With this in mind then, I'd like to talk to you today … about *Venus*.

(Pause.)

CHRISTIANA: You've already talked of your *pleasure*, and your *immediate availability*, and now you wish to talk of love! I didn't expect such an excess of … gallantry at our first meeting! But before I respond, could I persuade you, as resident physician here, to look at my legs?

DR. ORANGE: Your legs??

CHRISTIANA: *(Sighs.)* I've been in such pain all week!

DR. ORANGE: Where?

(She sits and pulls up long skirts and petticoats to reveal bare ankles.)

CHRISTIANA: Ankles. Mostly. And a little higher.

(Pause.)

DR. ORANGE: Describe the pain.

CHRISTIANA: Painful.

(He sits back in chair, folds arms and regards her with raised eyebrows. Eventually she lowers skirts.)

I'd hoped for an examination at least. You might have found out all about Venus.

DR. ORANGE: *(Sighs.)* If you won't talk about that, let's talk about what happened to you on the fourth of September 1870.

(Pause. CHRISTIANA becomes angry.)

CHRISTIANA: For heaven's sake, that was almost two years ago! It was a day like any other. How could I possibly remember?

DR. ORANGE: Do you deny saying what Matron clearly overheard?

CHRISTIANA: I won't deny Matron is a jealous little frump who wishes me ill.

(Pause. Doctor starts to put away papers.)

DR. ORANGE: I can see we will make no progress this morning. I am terminating this meeting. The habit of … secretiveness led directly to your crimes. We must break it to effect your cure. This is my duty and I will not flinch from it. I will see you at the same time next week and every week. I am sure that in time, we will begin to make progress. Have a good day, Miss Edmunds.

(CHRISTIANA exits office and goes over to where COLEMAN stands.)

CHRISTIANA: He allows me no privacy! And how can I talk about *love* to someone who's too frightened even to *dance!?* Oh, but he'd love me to dance naked for him! *'Dance for daddy Chrissie! My little dancing princess!'*

COLEMAN: 'E 'as to talk to you about your crime, Miss Edmunds. That's 'is job.

CHRISTIANA: Haven't they all declared me insane a dozen times over? Isn't that enough?

COLEMAN: But 'e wants to cure you.

CHRISTIANA: What cure is there for the madness of love?

(Tense pause. They stare at each other. Lights up on office. DR. ORANGE writing in a ledger.)

COLEMAN: *(To audience.)* Christiana's Broadmoor case notes date from that day. Right from the start, there was something about them …

DR. ORANGE: Christiana Edmunds is very vain and deceitful … prefers mystery and concealment and seems to deceive for the pure love of deception. She affects a youthful appearance and her manner and expression lies towards the sexual and amorous …

COLEMAN: Couldn't put my finger on what it was.

DR. ORANGE: Continues to paint and "get herself up" – but when visited by her mother, she omits the colour on her cheeks, sheds tears, and complains of the injustice and cruelty with which she is treated, and of the searching of her room.

COLEMAN: Bit monotonous, but it was more than that. Something about the angry little details …

DR. ORANGE: In the envelope of a letter addressed to her sister she had very ingeniously fastened a single scrap of paper covered with extremely small writing. In this communication she asked her sister to bring some articles of dress clandestinely at her next visit and referred to modes of applying paint to the face. Her love of deception is quite a mania.

COLEMAN: Later, I understood. She'd got under 'is skin! The man was as obsessed with 'er as I was!

DR. ORANGE: Silly and frivolous in the general tone of her conversation and behaviour. Is very vain, courts and desires attention and notoriety, pushes herself forward on all occasions, paints and tricks herself up for inspection and in almost her every act shows how little she appreciates the gravity of her crime or the position in which it has placed her.

COLEMAN: You'd probably 'ave to know the doctor to understand it, but this was probably the closest 'e ever got … to writing love letters. Weeks turned into months. My own obsession was gettin' worse. After every Social Committee meeting, I'd linger behind as long as I could just to be near 'er. I'd use the meetings to pass clothes and beauty aids to 'er from the outside, bypassing Matron. Took some stupid risks in doing that, so when I was summoned to the Doctor's office one morning, I thought that I'd probably been rumbled.

(Lights up on DR. ORANGE's office.)

DR. ORANGE: Mr. Coleman, I'm afraid there's a serious matter I need to talk to you about.

COLEMAN: Sir?

(Pause.)

DR. ORANGE: A bottle of spirits has been found hidden in the attendants' cloakroom.

COLEMAN: *(Beat.)* I see sir.

DR. ORANGE: It's an area that all the attendants use, but I think we know who the culprit is.

COLEMAN: We do?

DR. ORANGE: Although we've only found him drunk on duty once, we both know that Mr. Murphy is actually a persistent offender. I'm afraid his previous warning means that this is now a dismissal matter. Would you tell him that I want to see him here in my office immediately?

COLEMAN: That won't be necessary sir.

(Pause.)

The brandy's mine.

DR. ORANGE: *(Beat.)* Mr. Coleman, I'm at a loss for words. I wasn't aware you had a problem.

COLEMAN: I like to think it 'asn't interfered with my work sir.

DR. ORANGE: Your record has been exemplary, but you know better than anyone the regulations on drinking at work.

COLEMAN: Actually, I'd been off the drink for quite some time sir. But I've 'ad a particularly difficult couple of months.

DR. ORANGE: Anything I should know about?

(Pause.)

COLEMAN: A disappointment in love sir. Foolish thing, but for some reason, its 'it me 'ard.

DR. ORANGE: That's natural. You're not married. Something we both … have in common Mr. Coleman. And neither of us is getting any younger. No prospect of a happy outcome in the matter?

COLEMAN: None whatsoever sir.

DR. ORANGE: That must be painful.

COLEMAN: I can't deny it is sir, but to be honest, all I want in the world is for the lady concerned to be 'appy. I'd do anything for 'er.

DR. ORANGE: You're a good man Mr. Coleman. She is foolish to reject you. If you find yourself struggling to resist this temptation again, and it would help to talk about it, my door is always open.

COLEMAN: Thank you sir. I won't forget your kindness.

DR. ORANGE: I appreciate your honesty about matters today, but you'll have to consider this discussion as a formal warning. Any repetition and you'll face exactly the same penalty Mr. Murphy or anyone else would face.

COLEMAN: Perfectly understood, sir.

(DR. ORANGE returns to his ledger. COLEMAN comes downstage, takes out hip flask, swigs and gasps.)

I said I was *tryin'* to lay off the drink, not succeedin'. We're all entitled to some secrets. It'd crept up on me again. Like love. By now, I couldn't go five minutes without thinkin' of 'er and then the gnawing in my guts'd start. *(Drinks.)*

Months flew by. The Association's Annual meeting was approaching fast. So was the ball. The doctor was making no progress. Everyone was getting a bit … fraught.

(Lights up on office. COLEMAN hands DR. a letter.)

DR. ORANGE: Another complaint from Matron? About Miss Edmunds, no doubt?

COLEMAN: *(Beat.)* It's about … the hair, sir.

(Pause.)

DR. ORANGE: Hair!?

COLEMAN: Yes, sir.

DR. ORANGE: How was that smuggled in!?

COLEMAN: In a cushion, I believe sir.

DR. ORANGE: Why does she need hair!?

COLEMAN: For a … hairpiece of some kind.

DR. ORANGE: For the *ball*, no doubt! In a *cushion!?*

COLEMAN: Yes, sir.

(Pause.)

DR. ORANGE: I need to see it.

(Pause.)

COLEMAN: It's just … hair in a cushion, Dr. Orange. There's not a lot to see. Matron's already confiscated it.

DR. ORANGE: I want to see it!!

COLEMAN: Of course.

DR. ORANGE: It may be *relevant!*

COLEMAN: I'll 'ave it brought 'ere sir.

DR. ORANGE: I'm seeing Miss Edmunds one last time before I leave for London. If her nymphomania has not subsided,

I'll have to decide whether it's wise to allow her to attend the ball.

(Pause.)

COLEMAN: Sir, it's not customary to deny inmates access to social functions. Particularly someone serving on the Social Committee. It doesn't seem fair.

DR. ORANGE: Are you questioning my medical judgement?

COLEMAN: I wasn't aware dancing was a medical matter, sir.

(Tense pause.)

DR. ORANGE: Mr. Coleman, how is the problem you spoke to me of not so long ago? Have you succumbed to temptation? Or have you been more successful in curbing your urges?

COLEMAN: Thank you for your concern, sir. The problem is now fully under control.

DR. ORANGE: I'm glad to hear it. That will be all. Have the cushion sent up to me.

(COLEMAN exits. CHRISTIANA enters office. Lights up on both, angry and exasperated.)

CHRISTIANA: Of course Matron is offended! She'd be thoroughly miserable if I didn't offend her on a regular basis!

DR. ORANGE: It's not just Matron you've offended this time! For your own amusement, you've been secretly tormenting several of the more irritable inmates on your Ward.

CHRISTIANA: It's a diversion! It makes the Ward a far more lively and enjoyable place for everyone!

DR. ORANGE: *(Sighs.)* Miss Edmunds …

CHRISTIANA: I'm bored! And I'm angry about the outrages done to my privacy! The endless searches of my room and opening of my personal correspondence!

DR. ORANGE: As you very well know, this is normal procedure for all inmates, especially those in persistent breach of regulations.

CHRISTIANA: Are we ladies not entitled to some secrets? Aren't there things even in your life you'd rather not talk about?

DR. ORANGE: You're not entitled to secrecy about your crime! This is why you must tell me about Venus. It may be relevant.

(Pause.)

CHRISTIANA: How can I talk to you about love? How can you understand how unbearable it is to lose it, when you have so obviously never even felt it? You're clearly married to your job, although from what I see, the match is not a wholly happy one. Perhaps you should take a mistress?

DR. ORANGE: How many times? I will not respond to coquetry! Will you tell me what happened on the fourth of September 1870?

CHRISTIANA: How would I know!? Perhaps a handsome soldier smiled at me in the Royal Pavilion or I bought some material for a dress. The sun rose. The tide came in and went out again! The world did not come to an end!

DR. ORANGE: I have neither time nor patience for this! Do you understand the physical effects of strychnine on the human body?

(Pause. He takes book from shelf. CHRISTIANA looks away from him. He reads from book.)

Ten to twenty minutes after ingestion, the muscles in the head and neck begin to spasm resulting in lockjaw. Spasms soon spread to every muscle in the body, with continuous convulsions which increase in intensity and frequency until the backbone arches continually. The temperature of the body climbs uncontrollably because it cannot dissipate the heat caused by the seizures. The fitting progressively damages muscle and skeletal tissue, inflicting a series of injuries which are painfully exacerbated by every fresh convulsion. Death comes from asphyxiation caused by paralysis of the nerves that control breathing, or by sheer exhaustion from the convulsions. It is excruciatingly painful and terrifying and it is not quick. This whole process takes two to three hours. During that time, the slightest stimulus makes the convulsions worse, so attempts to comfort, such as the hand of a mother trying desperately to soothe her dying little boy will only add to his agonies.

(Long pause. CHRISTIANA slowly gets up, showing no sign of emotion.)

CHRISTIANA: *(Sighs.)* I had a childish dream that I would persuade you to dance and that you would amaze the whole of Broadmoor, and yourself. But you want me to dance naked while not even venturing onto the floor yourself. 'Dance Chrissie, dance! Earn your sweets!'

DR. ORANGE: A child lies dead, and you dare to talk about dancing!? And sweets!?

CHRISTIANA: I will not perform for you, father! I dance only for myself now!

DR. ORANGE: *(Furious.)* I am not your father! I have no children!

(Pause. DOCTOR struggles to collect himself.)

Miss Edmunds, you are clearly unwell. I think we should finish our meeting now. Matron will take you back to the Ward.

CHRISTIANA: Thank you doctor. I think that's best. I have so much to do still before the ball.

(She exits office quickly and goes offstage. Lights down on office, lights up on COLEMAN who comes slowly downstage to address audience. He first takes a deep swig from his flask.)

COLEMAN: On the morning of the ball, Dr. Orange left for 'is meeting in London and Matron informed Christiana that she would not be allowed to attend that evenin'. She went 'ysterical, and 'ad to be sedated and moved to the Infirmary. It's very close to the Central Hall where I was on duty that night for the ball.

(FX. Waltz music. He takes another swig.)

I kept imaginin' 'er wakin', an' 'earin' the music through the walls, an' goin' mad with it. I couldn't bear it. Soon after the ball started, I crept away an' went into the Infirmary. Christiana was the only woman in there that night. It was a crazy risk, goin' into the Women's section with no good reason, but I managed to duck into 'er room without being seen.

(CHRISTIANA enters in nightgown and gets onto bed with back to audience. Low light up on bed. COLEMAN stands as if in doorway watching her.)

She was lyin' on top of the covers. *(Gulps from flask.)* There was one high, barred window and moonlight was streamin' through it across 'er bed. Red hot embers were still burning in the grate, and the room was close and warm and full of the gorgeous smell of her. I closed my eyes and breathed it in. I opened them again. My face was wet with tears. Funny, I couldn't remember crying. *(Beat.)* 'Er nightdress was undone at the neck and … I could just see one breast partly exposed. I stood there starin', like a kid in a sweetshop. Don't know 'ow long it was. Then I leaned over and gently moved the collar of 'er nightdress down another inch.

(He moves nightdress. Audience cannot see what he can.)

A nipple. So soft and sweet and beautiful. I was tired, an' drunk, an' I'd never wanted anythin' so much in my life. She seemed so fast asleep with the laudanum I thought, if I was very quiet, and gentle …

(He kneels down, his face hidden behind her body, but it is clear what he is doing. He stays there a little while, then gets up again.)

I took it in my mouth. Just for that moment, the pain in my guts stopped. I felt peaceful and 'appy. She was still breathing slowly and deeply like she was asleep. But when I stood up and looked down, she was staring up at me. She smiled and whispered …

CHRISTIANA: Daddy?

(COLEMAN turns and starts to flee as she rouses.)

COLEMAN: Jesus!

CHRISTIANA: John?

(Pause. He stops, agonises.)

COLEMAN: Miss Edmunds?

CHRISTIANA: I must talk about what happened.

COLEMAN: What do you mean, Miss? Nothing happened!

CHRISTIANA: I know that's what Charles said, but he lied. I have to talk about it, don't I? Or I'll never be cured. I can't talk to Dr. Orange or Matron or any of them. You're the only person here I trust.

(Long pause. COLEMAN slowly comes and sits on bed.)

COLEMAN: Then talk to me.

(Fade down waltz music. She rises from the bed. DR. BEARD enters. The two of them act out the story.)

CHRISTIANA: September the fourth then.

DR. BEARD: Are you still sure you want to go through with it?

CHRISTIANA: We've tried not writing to each other, not seeing each other. I can't stop thinking about you.

DR. BEARD: Nor I about you, every waking second. It's a madness! At least this way, we'll finally know. You do believe that, don't you Chrissie?

CHRISTIANA: Yes! And you?

DR. BEARD: Of course! Book a hotel room. The Royal Albion would be best. I'll come straight to your room at eleven o'clock in the morning. If asked, I'm a doctor who's been called to treat a patient privately. We'll have until late afternoon. I can't take the risk of being away longer. We'll leave separately. It would be best if you stayed on in the room overnight to avert suspicion.

CHRISTIANA: Such meticulous planning Charles! Anyone would think you'd done this before!

(Her laughter trails awkwardly. Pause.)

DR. BEARD: Are you sure?

CHRISTIANA: Go! I'll see you in the Royal Albion!

(FX crashing sea and gulls wheeling.)

(To COLEMAN.) I walked along the seafront from the West Pier. The tide was coming in and the sea was monstrous and angry. Then I walked out along the Chain Pier and watched the waves smashing into the stone jetty there, spray and spume thrown up twenty feet into the air. So exhilarating! A fine mist dampened my clothes and my hair, and there was the sharp, metallic taste of the sea on my tongue. I could hardly bear to tear myself away, but eventually I did and I checked into the hotel late. Charles knocked at the door after I'd been in the room ten minutes.

(Fade down sea and gulls.)

DR. BEARD: Where in God's name were you?

CHRISTIANA: What's the matter?

DR. BEARD: We said eleven o'clock! I was here and you weren't in the room! A maid asked if I'd lost my key. I had to walk back out through Reception where everyone had seen me walk in a minute earlier. It drew attention to me! This is precisely what I wanted to avoid! You've embarrassed me!

CHRISTIANA: I'm so sorry! I was on the pier and the sea was so beautiful, and I lost track of time.

DR. BEARD: I almost didn't come back.

CHRISTIANA: You're here now.

(She puts her arms round him and kisses him. He does not respond. She turns away and looks out to the audience as through a window.)

DR. BEARD: You have to appreciate the … delicacy of my position, Christiana. Letters are one thing. This is of a completely different order.

CHRISTIANA: I'm well aware of that.

DR. BEARD: We're at a crossroads. This is the most serious decision of our lives.

CHRISTIANA: Do I have to listen to that speech again? I made my decision long ago. Otherwise what would I be doing here in this room with you?

DR. BEARD: Do you appreciate the risk to me of discovery? I'd be spurned by polite society and it would be impossible to practise medicine in Brighton.

CHRISTIANA: I know how to keep a secret! *(To COLEMAN.)* I'd never touched a man and now, I just wanted to get on with it! But he wanted to talk and talk about it.

(DR. BEARD mimes talking. Time is passing.)

After half an hour or so, I confess, I wasn't paying much attention. I kept looking at the engraving of Botticelli's 'Birth of Venus' on the wall by the window – and I was watching the strange shapes in the seaspray and listening to the surf roaring up and down the beach outside. Finally,

I couldn't bear to listen to him any longer. *(To DR. BEARD.)* Do you know the story of the birth of Venus?

DR. BEARD: What!? No. Is it terribly romantic?

CHRISTIANA: *(To COLEMAN.)* I told him.

DR. BEARD: Copulation, castration and murder! Charming!

CHRISTIANA: I like it!

DR. BEARD: Why!?

CHRISTIANA: I don't know.

DR. BEARD: You're a curious creature! What about the father? Poor old Uranus!

CHRISTIANA: Maybe he deserved it. *(To COLEMAN.)* And I listened to the sea, and saw shapes in the spray and I suddenly felt the universe shift and crack all around me, as if I were the ocean and a great whale was finally rising to the surface. And I realised that Venus had been reborn in me. *(To DR. BEARD.)* Yes, he must have deserved it!

DR. BEARD: Chrissie, are you all right?

CHRISTIANA: I don't want to talk any longer! That's not what we're here for!

(She kisses him passionately.)

DR. BEARD: You've … changed! What happened?

CHRISTIANA: I've become Venus. We will be afraid of nothing. There will be no more shame. Only two animals coming together in a frenzy! Touching …

DR. BEARD: Kissing …

CHRISTIANA: Licking …

DR. BEARD: Sniffing …

CHRISTIANA: Groaning …

DR. BEARD: Grunting …

CHRISTIANA: Ecstatic. I kissed his body all over, and he tasted …

DR. BEARD: Sweeter than the sweetest thing.

CHRISTIANA: We were drunk …

DR. BEARD: On each other …

CHRISTIANA: And we feasted …

DR. BEARD: All that day …

CHRISTIANA: Until the time came to part.

DR. BEARD: Oh, my Venus, born fresh from the sea!

(He hugs her, then takes a step away.)

CHRISTIANA: *(To COLEMAN.)* I'd never felt happier or more alive! Everything had changed. I looked out on the sea after he'd gone and watched a gull gliding through light and air and clouds. A perfect moment on a perfect day. September the fourth, 1870. And I knew I could die happy, feeling beloved.

(Pause. Doctor's manner changes.)

I heard nothing for a week. When I saw him again, he looked drawn and anxious.

DR. BEARD: There are more important things than my personal happiness. I cannot just be selfish. If only we had met before, many years ago. All this must now stop.

CHRISTIANA: *(Whispers.)* How can it stop?

DR. BEARD: We cannot be together Chrissie! Emily is … in the way.

CHRISTIANA: I understand. Please go now.

(Pause. DR BEARD exits.)

(To COLEMAN.) I knew what he really meant and what he was telling me to do. I didn't sleep or eat for many days. I thought perhaps Venus should go back into the sea and I walked down to the Pier many times and was on the point of casting myself into the water, but could not. Then one evening, there was a charity ball in the Chinese rooms at the Royal Pavilion, and I went, just to escape the stifling horror of another evening in the house with my mother. I walked into the Entrance Hall and saw Charles coming towards me with Emily.

(DR. BEARD enters. He and CHRISTIANA stop suddenly in shock, seeing each other, then act out her words.)

DR. BEARD: My God! The woman's following me now!

CHRISTIANA: I tried to duck into another room, but he'd seen me and his face went white. I saw them leave soon after.

DR. BEARD: It's nothing Emily. Just feeling a little unwell. If you don't mind, can we go?

(He goes to one side, but not offstage. CHRISTIANA is dancing around the stage.)

CHRISTIANA: I danced till I was giddy and drank champagne between dances. But everyone was looking at me and suddenly I felt naked. I left the ballroom and wandered through the building. A soldier followed me and took me by the arm into a darkened room. We didn't say a word. I took his manhood in my mouth and I gorged like a starving person at a banquet. After he left, one of the Chinese serpents in the room slithered down from a pillar and spoke to me in the shape of Charles.

(DR. BEARD comes forward whispering the serpent's words.)

DR. BEARD: *(Whispers.)* Venus out of the sea at Brighton! Love so purified you, you became immortal. And now you can prove it!

(Offers CHRISTIANA bag of chocolates. She hesitates.)

Have one!

CHRISTIANA: What are they?

DR. BEARD: *(Whispers.)* Chocolates injected with strychnine. Remember? Charles joked of killing fat Emily with them. Go home now. Eat a whole bagful! You won't die! Promise!

CHRISTIANA: I was sick for many days, feverish and lightheaded, but the poison couldn't kill me, so I knew the serpent was right. And afterwards he visited me in my room.

DR. BEARD: *(Whispers.)* You can give the poison to Emily now as Charles wished. It would be a loving act! Give her the same amount you took yourself. That way, the chocolates will decide which one of you is meant to be with Charles.

CHRISTIANA: But she didn't die either.

DR. BEARD: Emily was violently ill after eating some of the chocolates you gave her. In God's name, what were you thinking of? Are you insane Christiana?

CHRISTIANA: I bought the same chocolates for myself from Maynards and have spent the whole weekend ill in bed. I was affected far worse than Emily!

DR. BEARD: You want to destroy me? Is that it? I'll tell them you're mad and nothing happened between us. You won't break Emily and I up. The poisoning has only brought us closer!

CHRISTIANA: Of course, this was confusing at first, but the serpent explained everything later.

DR. BEARD: *(Whispers.)* You did nothing wrong. The poison brought them closer. A gift of love. Love's sweet poison burns away what ties us to earth and sets us free. What's left of us is light and air and clouds. It would be a beautiful thing, don't you think? To give out the gift of love to everyone?

(DR. BEARD exits.)

CHRISTIANA: And that's what I did for many months before I came here.

COLEMAN: But a child died Christiana. Sidney Barker.

(Pause.)

CHRISTIANA: You think I don't know what terrible things happen to children?

(Pause. COLEMAN approaches her.)

COLEMAN: Did something happen … to you?

CHRISTIANA: Nothing happened!

COLEMAN: All right!

(Pause.)

CHRISTIANA: You actually care, don't you?

COLEMAN: Yes.

(Pause. She smiles, reaches out and touches his cheek.)

CHRISTIANA: Do you think I haven't noticed how you've been looking at me all these months? The excuses to spend time with me? All the little kindnesses? Do you think I haven't felt your loneliness? Do you think I don't feel the same?

COLEMAN: Chrissie …

CHRISTIANA: Oh John! I've told you everything now! Such a relief! Dr. Orange was right. Secretiveness was poisoning me! And now that I've spoken, perhaps a cure is possible?

COLEMAN: Of course it is! That's all that everyone wants for you.

CHRISTIANA: Do you want it? Specially?

COLEMAN: Yes.

CHRISTIANA: Then kiss me.

(She edges towards him on the bed. Takes his face in her hands as if to kiss him. At last minute he stops her.)

I understand. I can wait. Anyway, you've already shown your true feelings unashamedly here tonight. What a relief after all these months!

(Shocked pause. COLEMAN frightened and formal.)

COLEMAN: I think there may 'ave been some mistake, Miss.

CHRISTIANA: *(Laughs.)* What!?

COLEMAN: You've been very heavily sedated and under the influence of laudanum, Miss. It sounds to me like you may 'ave imagined something.

CHRISTIANA: John!

COLEMAN: Such an accusation would completely destroy me!

CHRISTIANA: But it was beautiful! I felt such love for you at that moment. Suckling you as if you were my own darling child.

(Pause.)

COLEMAN: Miss Edmunds, nothing happened. And the only child who should be in your thoughts is Sidney Barker.

(Pause. She draws back. Her manner hardens.)

CHRISTIANA: Perhaps I'd better get some sleep, so that the laudanum can wear off and I'll be able to see and understand things more clearly.

(Lights down. CHRISTIANA goes offstage. Lights up on office and DR. ORANGE who has clearly been drinking.)

COLEMAN: You asked to see me, sir?

DR. ORANGE: What's your poison, Mr. Coleman! Brandy, isn't it?

(He pours a drink from a decanter on his desk and then forgets to give it to COLEMAN.)

COLEMAN: This feels a little … uncomfortable, sir.

DR. ORANGE: Yes, Broadmoor's full of contradictions, isn't it? Attendants found with drink face summary dismissal, but the Superintendent has a stock, paid for by the institution, to entertain guests. Today, you're my guest. God knows, I need company.

COLEMAN: Sir?

DR. ORANGE: I'm sorry. The meeting yesterday. I don't know why it's affected me so much.

COLEMAN: What went wrong?

DR. ORANGE: My speech! Maudsley watched me the whole time, sneering while I stumbled and my mouth dried. When I finished, he yawned, got up to speak and forensically demolished everything I'd said. 'Not a shred of truth in these sentimental claims for the asylums! Insane population has been growing steadily for twenty years! The evidence is that asylums make many inmates worse!

COLEMAN: But you've always said Maudsley was 'alf mad 'imself sir! The wild-eyed prophet of doom, remember?

DR. ORANGE: He said 'our destiny is made by inheritance. The insane are a degenerate subspecies of humanity, mostly incurable.' And as I listened, do you know what I felt? Relief! I realised why my speech felt like a complete fraud. Madness is as wild and fathomless as the sea. Our business isn't cure. It's containment.

COLEMAN: I don't believe that! I'm sure you don't really, sir.

DR. ORANGE: What if I do? What am I to think of the life I've led, married to this job? Without love. Without children. Forgive me, Mr. Coleman. I don't know why I'm being so maudlin.

COLEMAN: *(Mutters.)* Because you're drunk.

DR. ORANGE: Hmmm? *(Drinks.)* Did anything ever happen with the lady you once mentioned?

COLEMAN: Absolutely nothing happened, sir. It was for the best.

DR. ORANGE: Sad to hear it nevertheless. *(Drinks.)* How did the ball go?

COLEMAN: Well enough, sir.

DR. ORANGE: Was Miss Edmunds quiet in the night?

(COLEMAN takes the drink intended for him. Gulps it.)

COLEMAN: Afraid not sir. Very distressed when she came round from the laudanum. I went into the Infirmary to try and 'elp calm 'er, but 'er speech was confused and full of sexual references. Gave an account of an incident at a charity ball in the Royal Pavilion where she committed a lewd act with a soldier, a complete stranger she met in a darkened room.

DR. ORANGE: *(Sighs. Shakes head.)* Gods! I'm going to discontinue the meetings. I was naïve to think talking could achieve anything. Her father died in an asylum. Inheritance! Maudsley's right. What chance did the poor girl have?

COLEMAN: Yes sir.

DR. ORANGE: *(Drinks.)* I cannot get the suffering of that little boy out of my mind. The times I've sat in this office and raged and wept as if I'd lost my own child. And she's still not aware she's done anything wrong! The pity of it is almost unbearable. Another drink, Mr. Coleman?

COLEMAN: I'll leave you to it, Sir. I need to get back.

(Lights down on office. DR. ORANGE exits. COLEMAN comes downstage to address audience.)

And I 'aven't touched a drop since. Don't know 'ow long it'll last this time, but I terrified myself that night. What else was I capable of? She asked to see me from time to time, but I ignored the requests, or sent excuses. Eventually, she gave up. That, and my discrediting 'er with the doctor made a cowardly, shameful end to the business. I went through agonies, not seein' 'er, but I was frightened of losing my job, and I discovered in the end that the cure for love is fear. I needn't 'ave worried about Christiana. She kept my secret, like she kept all the others, which only made me feel worse.

Venus appeared out of the sea at Brighton and swept through all these lives like a tidal wave. Most of us got off lightly. Broken 'earts are ten a penny. But when the waters subsided, there was a tiny broken body washed up on Brighton beach. An innocent child who died in agony to show the madness of love. A sacrifice. I can't bear to think about it too much. But when I do, I try to remember what Christiana said about having a perfect moment on a perfect day and knowing you could die happy, feeling beloved. I had my moment. With every ounce of my strength now, I keep wishing, imagining and dreaming a moment like that for Sidney Barker. It helps.

(Music 'Venus'. DR. BEARD, DR. ORANGE and CHRISTIANA enter. They act out the scene as before, but more slowly and feelingly.)

DR. BEARD: *(As Uncle Charlie.)* What'll it be then little Sidney?

COLEMAN: *(As Sidney.)* I can't make up my mind, uncle Charlie!

DR. BEARD: *(As Uncle Charlie.)* Come on, lad! You'll have to go soon! Your mum and dad are waiting! We've got a train to catch!

COLEMAN: *(As Sidney.)* All right! *(Beat.)* What are those?

DR. BEARD: *(As Uncle Charlie.)* Chocolate creams?

CHRISTIANA: He knows they're expensive. Not like the cheap confectionery he's used to …

DR. BEARD: Boiled sweets …

CHRISTIANA: Sherberts …

DR. BEARD: Liquorice …

CHRISTIANA: Special! A whole new world of sweetness and pleasure.

COLEMAN: *(As Sidney.)* Chocolate creams please, Uncle Charlie!

CHRISTIANA: On the way back to the train station a pretty lady with a parasol smiles at him and he smiles back.

DR. ORANGE: He counts up all the good things in the day.

COLEMAN: The train journey.

DR. BEARD: The donkey ride on the beach.

COLEMAN: Makin' the sandcastles.

DR. ORANGE: Paddling in a warm sea.

CHRISTIANA: Running all the way to the end of Chain Pier, through the seaspray of the big waves.

DR. BEARD: He smiles up at Uncle Charlie, pops a chocolate cream into his mouth and feels it flood with an unfamiliar sweetness.

CHRISTIANA: He'll have to go soon. But he knows he'll remember this moment forever. A perfect end to a perfect day.

DR. ORANGE: Sunshine …

DR. BEARD: The endless sea …

COLEMAN: The waves crashin' onto the sand …

CHRISTIANA: And blue sky stretching into the distance …

DR. BEARD: Forever.

COLEMAN: Light …

DR. ORANGE: And air …

CHRISTIANA: And clouds.

(Pause. Music louder. Fade slowly to black.)

THE DEMON BOX

O, wonder!
How many goodly creatures are there here?
How beauteous mankind is! O brave new world,
That has such people in't.

The Tempest

'The Demon Box' is dedicated to Robert Dadd,
apothecary and amateur geologist
(1789–1843)

Characters

RICHARD DADD (1817–86)
Artist. At Broadmoor, 1865–86.

DR. WILLIAM CHESTER MINOR (1834–1920)
Surgeon in American Civil War and
lexicographer on first Oxford English
Dictionary. At Broadmoor, 1872–1910.

MR. COLEMAN
Principal attendant, Block 2, Broadmoor.

ARIEL
A spirit

SET

A section of the back of the dropcloth or drop curtain that Dadd is painting is visible near front of stage. Nearby is a stool and a small table on which stands some paints, rag, brushes, a bowl of water, a fossil and teacups. On other side of stage is an easel with a small painting on it. There is a large coffin-sized crate on castors which can be moved around the stage and is big enough to hold a person. It can be lit from within and one side has a translucent fabric panel that a face can press through. Another side has strange, hieroglyph-like designs on.

HISTORICAL NOTE

After a promising start to his career as an artist, Richard Dadd began to show signs of serious mental disturbance during a trip to Egypt in 1841. Upon his return, believing himself to be under instruction from the god Osiris, he murdered his father. He spent the rest of his life in asylums, first Bethlem Hospital and then Broadmoor. While inside, he spent nine years working on the oil painting regarded as his masterpiece, 'The Fairy Feller's Master Stroke'. He later completed a watercolour copy in Broadmoor. In 1872 Dr. William Chester Minor and Christiana Edmunds were admitted to Broadmoor and Richard Dadd was asked to decorate the theatre there. Part of this job was a painted drop curtain, entitled 'The Temple of Fame'. This has not survived, but there is a detailed sketch of the design.

(Preset. Eerie lighting. DADD alone on stage painting drop curtain. Echoing soundscape of whispers, fairy laughter, wind, running water and rain. ARIEL hops, somersaults and gambols onto stage. She perches, hunched up and watches him curiously, head on one side. MINOR is reading from a book. Red light up on COLEMAN who takes a chocolate cream from a bag and studies it.)

COLEMAN: The summer of 1872, and I was tryin' to lay off the drink, so I 'ad my sweet tooth back, an' the craving for my old favourites. But then Christiana Edmunds was admitted, the Chocolate Cream Poisoner, and I fell in love with 'er, and these never tasted quite the same again. Oh Chrissie …

(Puts chocolate away again.)

But that's another story. And you've not come to Broadmoor to 'ear about me. I've not murdered anyone! Yet. Please, Mr. Dadd, the actors are ready to go on stage!

DADD: They'll have to wait!

COLEMAN: *(To Audience.)* For some months now Mr. Richard Dadd 'as been *beautifying* the theatre 'ere at Broadmoor. Big job!

DADD: Murals for all the walls, panels under the stage, and a huge canvas for the drop curtain entitled 'The Temple of Fame.'

COLEMAN: Problem is, 'e insisted 'is curtain 'ad to be painted *onstage*.

DADD: To see what works best in the space!

COLEMAN: The Broadmoor Players are not 'appy! They wanna start rehearsals …

DADD: They'll have to rehearse in the concert hall! It's not finished, and it can't be moved!

COLEMAN: All right! But you'll need to get a move on! What's the time now? *(Looks at Pocket Watch.)* May! About the time Dr. William Chester Minor was admitted.

MINOR: Former surgeon in American Civil War! Scholar and amateur artist!

COLEMAN: Rushed out of lodgings in Lambeth one evening earlier this year and shot dead a complete stranger called George Merrett.

MINOR: I can explain about the shooting!

COLEMAN: Didn't take 'im long to 'ear that Richard Dadd was a patient.

MINOR: The artist? He's a fellow of the Royal Academy!

COLEMAN: Yeah, yeah, 'e's a bloody genius! *(To Audience.)* Friendship's rare in 'ere. But part of my job is coaxin' people out of their box. I 'oped these two might get along.

MINOR: We have shared interests!

COLEMAN: Paintin' …

MINOR: Egyptology …

COLEMAN: Homicide … The doctor soon 'eard Mr. Dadd was workin' on the theatre.

MINOR: I love painting! And I love the theatre!

COLEMAN: An' I saw … an opportunity. *(To MINOR.)* Only thing is, it's goin' a bit slow. I think 'e needs some 'elp.

MINOR: You think he might take … an apprentice?

COLEMAN: Let's see! Get to know 'im! Chat! About that book you're reading!

MINOR: Egyptology!

COLEMAN: *(To Audience.)* I 'ad another motive. For twenty nine years, Mr. Dadd 'ad been saying an Egyptian god told 'im to murder 'is father.

DADD: Osiris put symbols in the sky over the temples at Karnak to explain. The demon to be killed was not really my father.

COLEMAN: If you're ever going to be cured, we need to *understand* a little more about that, Mr. Dadd. *(To Audience.)* Per'aps Dr. Minor could'elp. A bit of Egyptology an' I might decipher the hieroglyphics. Alas, the doctor's interest was a bit … specialised!

(MINOR goes to back of stage, with book in one hand and with back to audience, begins to masturbate.)

MINOR: The god Atum appeared first out of the void and to relieve his loneliness, he made love to his fist, ejaculated in his hand and drank his own semen to impregnate himself. This created Shu and Tefnut, the first god and goddess, and they were the parents of Isis, Set and Osiris of the Mysteries. And of all creation.

DADD: *(Whispers.)* Creation!

COLEMAN: That's lovely, Dr. Minor. But would you look up *Osiris* when you've finished?

MINOR: And the flooding of the Nile results from the ejaculation of a river god called *Hapy*!

COLEMAN: Wasn't 'e one of the seven dwarves?

MINOR: Divine self love brought everything into existence!

COLEMAN: The Super Dr. Orange said we'd 'ave to stop all that. You'll stop the sun risin' first sir, I said. What's the time now? *(Looks at Pocket Watch.)* June! Get a move on Mr. Dadd – God made the world in seven days! Oh, knock it on the head, Dr. Minor!

(DADD steps back from drop curtain.)

DADD: Creation!

MINOR: Creation!

(MINOR roars his orgasm, turns round and throws handful of shiny confetti across small painting on easel. ARIEL tumbles forward as if thrown out of painting. Examines herself curiously.)

ARIEL: Created!

(Lighting change.)

COLEMAN: Dr. Minor did look it up. Apparently Osiris married his sister Isis, but their brother Set was jealous and tricked him into climbing inside a box. Then Set nails the lid shut, chucks it in the Nile and drowns 'im. Isis gets the coffin back, and is all for bringing him back to life, but Set turns up again, hacks the body into fourteen pieces and scatters 'em all over the world. *(Beat.)* Family life, eh? Tha's very 'elpful, Dr. Minor.

MINOR: Don't mention it!

COLEMAN: I'm beginning to see 'ow some of the pieces fit together. Wha's the time now? *(Looks at Pocket Watch.)* July! So slow! *(To MINOR.)* Mr. Dadd works on a different clock to the rest of us. 'E spent nine years workin' on that fairy painting at Bedlam.

DADD: *(Laughs.)* The years felt like days.

COLEMAN: An' the first thing 'e did when 'e got to Broadmoor?

DADD: The watercolour copy? That only took a year!

MINOR: Such concentration! Discipline!

COLEMAN: More bloody-mindedness, I always thought.

DADD: An artist has to make sacrifices.

COLEMAN: 'E still keeps it in 'is room.

MINOR: Could I possibly … see it?

COLEMAN: I'm sorry Doctor, but 'e 'ates people in 'is room, an' e'd go berserk if 'e ever found out. What's the matter?

MINOR: He's not someone who'll ever take an apprentice!

COLEMAN: You've got to winkle 'im out of his shell!

MINOR: I've tried! He won't even talk with me!

COLEMAN: Keep tryin'!

MINOR: The days here already feel like years! Every waking second thinking 'How am I to fill all this time?' I had such a dream last night, Mr. Coleman! I was pregnant with some kind of monster. I knew I'd give birth to him and then he'd devour me! Is this my future?

COLEMAN: *(Beat.)* Come with me. I'll show you the paintin'.

(Lighting change. While DADD continues to work on drop curtain, COLEMAN and MINOR cross to easel, COLEMAN looking nervously around.)

'E's gone to work on the curtain. Come on in, but be careful!

ARIEL: *(Whispers to DADD.)* People go into your room when you're not there, move your brushes, smudge the canvas!

(MINOR moves a brush. COLEMAN bumps into the canvas and smudges it.)

COLEMAN: Bugger!

MINOR: My God! How to describe it?

(Projections of 'the fairy feller'. ACTORS become the painting. Green lighting. Noise of whirring crickets.)

DADD: The middle of a wood …

MINOR: In the undergrowth …

ARIEL: Stalks of grass, towering like trees …

COLEMAN: Giant jungle leaves …

DADD: And strewn across the forest floor …

ARIEL: Acorns …

COLEMAN: 'Azelnuts …

MINOR: A splatter of dark seeds …

ARIEL: Like strange, ancient rocks …

MINOR: Each one perfect.

ARIEL: A germ of everything that is to be.

DADD: Like an idea for a painting.

COLEMAN: An' just look at this weird crowd!

MINOR: Nobles …

DADD: Ladies …

ARIEL: Fairies …

COLEMAN: Goblins …

MINOR: Dwarves …

ARIEL: A midget witch …

DADD: A cross-eyed elf …

MINOR: Apothecary …

DADD: No, alchemist!

COLEMAN: A little demon, peerin' up that woman's skirt!

DADD: Mysterious Patriarch, or God …

COLEMAN: An' right in the middle …

MINOR: With his back to you …

ARIEL: And his axe raised …

COLEMAN: A woodcutter.

DADD: No, fairy feller!

(They come out of the painting.)

MINOR: The colours are so intense, yet frozen somehow, as if drained of light. The whole scene seems to take place inside a dark, sunless box.

COLEMAN: When 'e first showed it me, I asked 'im – what's it about then?

DADD: The Mysteries of Osiris. Plutarch considers some of the Osiris cult rituals too sacred to even describe. He says, 'I pass over the cutting of the wood.'

COLEMAN: Another hieroglyphic. I didn't like the sound of it, but I didn't really know what to say. *(To DADD.)* I like all the different … creatures.

DADD: You can't see all of them.

COLEMAN: Really?

DADD: I've imprisoned many invisible ones in the painting, my little fairy helpers. They complete tasks for me and then I let them go, like Prospero releasing Ariel. Put that in your notes.

(COLEMAN crosses back to MINOR at easel.)

COLEMAN: Yeah, right. *(To Audience.) Weird talk* was a way of sayin' go away and let me paint.

DADD: Correct.

(MINOR is lost in picture. COLEMAN crosses back to MINOR.)

COLEMAN: It's about the Mysteries of Osiris, 'e said. What do you think 'e meant?

MINOR: Human sacrifice.

COLEMAN: *(Looking at painting again.)* Jesus!

MINOR: That such flowers can bloom in this place! Now my disappointment that he will not let me in is even greater.

COLEMAN: Just keep talkin' to 'im!

MINOR: I told you, I tried! Earlier today, out in the recreation yard.

COLEMAN: Don't give up!

MINOR: But he didn't even hear what I was saying! He looked right through me as if I were invisible.

(Lighting change. Exit MINOR and COLEMAN.)

DADD: Don't think I can't see you.

ARIEL: No one else sees me. Or hears me.

DADD: I hear every word. But you're not like the others.

ARIEL: A demon? No.

DADD: I don't believe in fairies.

ARIEL: What about spirits? Don't you recognise me?

DADD: *(Peers.)* Ariel!?

ARIEL: Now do you believe?

DADD: I don't know.

ARIEL: You should. You created me. Out of light and air and clouds.

DADD: Shakespeare created you.

ARIEL: But you made me real. To relieve your loneliness.

DADD: *(Sobs.)* Did I?

ARIEL: There now! Hush! Waited a long time for me, haven't you?

DADD: Bedlam and Broadmoor. Twenty-nine years.

ARIEL: Twenty-nine years of demons. But I'm here now.

DADD: … Ariel was …

ARIEL: Male? We spirits shift shape. It makes eternity more interesting. I can change back if this form is … unpleasing.

DADD: It's not … unpleasing.

ARIEL: Good! *(Beat.)* You have work for me?

(ARIEL inspects the drop curtain.)

DADD: *(Sighs.)* So much still to do.

ARIEL: Shall I click my fingers and it will be done? I can!

'What shall I do? Say what? What shall I do?'

DADD: *(Laughs.)* Keep me company while I work. Tell me your story.

(ARIEL picks up fossil ammonite from table.)

ARIEL: That would take a long time. Do you know how old this rock is?

DADD: Permian basalt. Two hundred and fifty million years. A *gift* from the demon calling itself 'father'.

ARIEL: *(Imitates father's voice.)* Apothecary and amateur geologist!

DADD: *(Laughs. Imitates father's voice.)* This tiny fossil alone is old enough to disprove the existence of all the gods!

ARIEL: *(Laughs.)* But then you sent him on the way to becoming a fossil himself.

DADD: Of his bones are coral made!

ARIEL: His fossil disproves nothing! Before there were people, or rocks, or an earth, there were spirits, like me. And gods.

DADD: Osiris of the Mysteries!

ARIEL: And his sister Isis whom he married, and his brother Set who murdered him with a magic box.

DADD: That's what they should be showing on this stage!

ARIEL: What will they show instead?

DADD: A comedy about some idiot falling in love probably. *(Sarcastically.)* What fun!

ARIEL: And it could be more!

DADD: So much more!

ARIEL: Elementals!

DADD: Monsters!

ARIEL: Angels!

DADD: Demons!

ARIEL: Gods! And that's why you take so much time and trouble over this theatre. The gods love you for that.

DADD: It doesn't feel that way sometimes.

ARIEL: That's because sometimes you shut them out. You have to let them in. Remember they were *your* family, in another life, just as I was.

(Pause. Lighting change. Music.)

DADD: Isis …

ARIEL: Osiris …

DADD: Happily married …

ARIEL: Brother …

DADD: Sister …

ARIEL: Twins! Who loved …

DADD: Even in the womb!

ARIEL: Wife …

DADD: And husband …

ARIEL: In the marshlands.

DADD: At the Nile delta. At the beginning of time.

ARIEL: Where millions of spirits sleep invisible

Among the bullrushes! All whispering …

DADD: *(Whisper.)* Osiris!

ARIEL: Be my god.

(It seems they might kiss, but DADD pulls away. Lighting change, music stops.)

DADD: Aren't those Caliban's words?

ARIEL: *(Claps.)* Very good, Richard! And you wouldn't want to go kissing *him*, would you?

DADD: But you are Ariel?

ARIEL: You should know. You created me. Out of light and air and clouds … and Shakespeare! *(Approaches him.)*

All hail, great master! Grave sir, hail! I come

To answer thy best pleasure!

DADD: My brave spirit! I have work for you!

ARIEL: What shall I do? Say what? What shall I do?

DADD: I … *(Sadly.)* I can't remember what comes next.

(Pause.)

ARIEL: The new American patient. The irritating one who keeps trying to talk to you …

DADD: … about Egypt? He seems genuine.

ARIEL: Your father seemed human.

DADD: … What do you think?

ARIEL: Perhaps I should … observe him?

DADD: Observe him closely! Report back on what you see!

ARIEL: I will be correspondent to command

And do my spiriting gently.

DADD: Do so, and after a time, I will discharge thee.

ARIEL: Aahh! So we have … a bargain?

DADD: Yes!

ARIEL: Kind master! I go!

(Lighting change. MINOR and COLEMAN enter.)

MINOR: He observed me so closely, it felt like I might be the model for his next painting!

COLEMAN: Persistence, see? Like I said.

MINOR: And he paid such attention to what I was saying! We talked about Egypt!

COLEMAN: Good! I'd like to hear a bit more about that sometime. For the notes. And now you've written 'im a letter?

(He hands COLEMAN letter and a small painting. COLEMAN skims through.)

… 'umbly beg you consider me … in the tradition of the masters … as apprentice for the studio of Richard Dadd … example of work attached.'

(COLEMAN crosses to where DADD works on drop curtain. DADD is already reading the letter.)

It would be a great kindness, Mr. Dadd. 'E's new and knows no one 'ere.

(DADD holds out hand silently and COLEMAN gives him painting. ARIEL cranes over his shoulder to look at it. She winces and shakes head solemnly.)

'E could paint in a bit of sea or somethin'? Sky! Can't be that difficult?

(DADD shakes his head over painting, hands back and resumes work.)

A word of encouragement for 'im, at least?

DADD: He has … potential!

ARIEL: But no real talent. *(Whispers.)* And can he be trusted?

(Lighting change. COLEMAN crosses back to MINOR and hands painting to him.)

MINOR: He thinks I have no real talent.

COLEMAN: 'E didn't say that!

MINOR: He didn't have to.

COLEMAN: 'E sees … potential. But 'e won't take on an apprentice just yet.

(Pause. MINOR examining his hands and arms.)

MINOR: I think the monster will not wait to be born. He'll grow out through my flesh. In the mornings now, I check every inch of my body, to see if it has begun. I can feel him moving beneath the surface of the skin. The first sign will be markings there. Symbols. Any day now.

COLEMAN: That's not gonna happen! Look at me, Dr. Minor! Don't give up! Mr. Dadd might still let you in!

MINOR: How!?

COLEMAN: *(Sighs.)* 'Ere's a thought – next Wednesday …

ARIEL: How old are you?

COLEMAN: … is 'is birthday. *(Beat.)* It's worth a try.

MINOR: Yes! I will send him a special present!

DADD: Almost fifty-four.

ARIEL: No. How old are you *really*?

DADD: … I can't remember. Tell me.

ARIEL: Before there were people, or rocks, or an earth, billions of years ago, Atum sprayed his seed across the empty canvas of the heavens. Like paint. You were there. Don't you remember? Happy birthday.

(MINOR wheels on large box and leaves card.)

Oh. Someone has left you a gift!

DADD: *(Reads card.)* 'Happy birthday Mr. Dadd. In most hands, this *box* would be quite useless, but in the hands of a true wizard, O what magic! Should the *sorcerer* ever change his mind about needing an *apprentice* …'

(Lighting change. MINOR and COLEMAN freeze.)

ARIEL: *(Whispers.)* The Murder Box!

DADD: What?

ARIEL: The present Set gave to Osiris!

DADD: The American is Set!?

ARIEL: You set me to observe him! You must have suspected!

DADD: It says 'from an admirer'.

ARIEL: *(Sarcastic.)* He wants to be your *friend.*

DADD: What shall I say to him!?

ARIEL: That he has no real talent.

DADD: Wouldn't that be *cruel*?

ARIEL: You know what happened when Osiris accepted a gift.

DADD: I can't remember.

ARIEL: Learn his lesson now then. And remember it well.

(ARIEL turns box round so that symbols face outwards. Lighting change. They act out the myth.)

DADD: Isis …

ARIEL: Osiris …

DADD: Happily married …

ARIEL: Brother …

DADD: Sister …

ARIEL: Twins! Who loved …

DADD: Even in the womb!

ARIEL: Wife …

DADD: And husband …

(It seems they might kiss, but ARIEL pulls away. MINOR unfreezes.)

ARIEL: … invite their brother Set …

DADD: To a feast.

MINOR: Brother! Thank you for inviting me. Truly, we live in the Golden Age. All the world is young, you and Isis rule wisely, there is harmony in the universe. I feel not a shred of jealousy! No! I rejoice in your good fortune, your greatness, your genius! And to mark this occasion, I bring you a present.

DADD: What is it?

MINOR: A kind of *party novelty*, a *box*!

DADD: Look Isis! What fun!

MINOR: Yes, a kind of box. Let's call it … oohhh, I don't know … The Osiris Box! In your honour. It's magical. Only one person in the whole world can fit exactly inside it.

ARIEL: Dearest one, I don't want you to go inside Set's box.

MINOR: Too small and the box will spit them out. Too large and we cannot close the lid.

ARIEL: Beloved, I don't want them to close the lid on you.

MINOR: But once the right person is inside the box, he will find a doorway.

ARIEL: You mustn't go through any doorway!

MINOR: Silly Isis! A woman's heart! No stomach for adventure!

DADD: Where will the doorway lead?

MINOR: Only the person who fits exactly inside the box can tell us that! And no one has succeeded … yet.

DADD: *(To ARIEL.)* Do I have to?

ARIEL: Learn the lesson of Osiris.

(DADD climbs inside box. COLEMAN unfreezes, and starts making notes. MINOR talks to COLEMAN, ARIEL to DADD's coffin.)

COLEMAN: Then Set *nails the lid shut* and chucks it in the Nile!

ARIEL: Poor Osiris was drowned.

MINOR: And that was how Death entered the world.

COLEMAN: Then Isis gets the coffin back, but Set turns up again, 'acks the body into fourteen pieces and scatters 'em all over the world!? What 'appened next?

MINOR: Isis searches …

ARIEL: through the whole of Egypt …

MINOR: And finds all the pieces …

ARIEL: washes them clean with her tears …

MINOR: And finds a suitable place

ARIEL: to bury him …

MINOR: But she wants to sleep with him …

ARIEL: one last time …

MINOR: So the god Ra breathes life back into Osiris …

ARIEL: for just one night …

MINOR: Isis puts the pieces together …

ARIEL: but one is missing …

MINOR: She fashions a penis of gold for the missing part.

ARIEL: And she enjoys one last night of love with her husband.

MINOR: The next day, Osiris dies again …

ARIEL: Anubis helps her embalm his body …

MINOR: and he becomes the first mummy …

ARIEL: awaiting rebirth.

MINOR: And to commemorate all this, forever afterwards …

ARIEL: into every tomb in Egypt was placed …

MINOR: The *Grain Osiris* …

ARIEL: *The Osiris Box* …

MINOR: A small box in the shape of the god …

ARIEL: Filled with Nile mud and dark seeds …

MINOR: That germinate in the grave.

ARIEL: To show that Osiris is the force driving the grain …

MINOR: And the Nile's rising flood waters …

ARIEL: And the daily resurrection of the sun.

MINOR: That you can kill him …

ARIEL: But he cannot die.

MINOR: Is that … helpful, Mr. Coleman?

COLEMAN: Them *Egyptians* got a lot to answer for! Thanks for that Dr. Minor, *(To audience.)* Though I'm not sure it brings us any closer to understanding why …e did it.

(Lighting change. MINOR and COLEMAN freeze.)

ARIEL: Nothing of him that doth fade …

DADD: Please, let me out! I'm not dead!

(ARIEL opens the box. DADD gets out.)

ARIEL: Did you find the doorway?

DADD: It was a trick!

ARIEL: The gods play tricks.

DADD: There was no way out!

ARIEL: They've locked you away here too.

DADD: As if I'd died.

ARIEL: And the Art Union journal called you …

DADD: The *late* Richard Dadd.

ARIEL: Many wish you dead! Be careful whom you trust. Like the American. Concentrate … on painting.

(She guides him back to his place at the drop curtain.)

People and things are not always what they seem. Remember your father.

DADD: Who *can* I believe!

ARIEL: You believe in me now, don't you?

DADD: Yes.

ARIEL: Then you will not die.

DADD: I will paint.

ARIEL: Happy birthday! But as for gifts, remember Osiris.

DADD: I won't ever forget again!

(Lighting change. COLEMAN unfreezes.)

COLEMAN: 'Appy birthday Mr. Dadd! An admirer of your work 'as sent you a special present, to 'elp with the great task.

(DADD carries on painting.)

Well aren't you goin' to open it? Dr. Minor went to a lot of trouble to get these sent in.

(COLEMAN makes to open it.)

DADD: Don't!

COLEMAN: It's paints, Mr. Dadd. Enough to last a lifetime. A very expensive gift.

DADD: I can't use them!

COLEMAN: That's a criminal waste!

DADD: And I don't need an apprentice!

COLEMAN: The poor bugger's just been admitted. Remember what your first few weeks were like? 'Ole life stretching ahead of you. Nothin' to fill the time. Not a friend in the world.

DADD: I remember nothing of that.

COLEMAN: You must remember something!

DADD: I remember Atum spraying seed across the heavens at the beginning of time and being with Isis in the marshes at the Nile Delta.

COLEMAN: Yeah right, and I suppose the bloody fairies are goin' to 'elp you finish the curtain.

DADD: Of course! Why there's one over by the paints eager to get on with the work. Ariel!

(Lighting change. ARIEL gambols across.)

ARIEL: Is there more toil? Since thou dost give me pains,

Let me remember thee what thou hast promised,

Which is not yet perform'd me.

DADD: How now? Moody?

What is't thou canst demand?

ARIEL: My liberty.

DADD: Liberty! Before the time be out? No more!

(She gambols off again. Lighting change. COLEMAN slow handclaps.)

COLEMAN: Very good. You ought to be on the stage. But you're not goin' to live forever, Mr. Dadd.

DADD: Oh, I don't know!

COLEMAN: An' the Broadmoor Players are waitin' for their theatre back an' givin' me a lot of grief. An' of course you can't be 'eld responsible, 'cos you're mad! So it's me 'oo'll get it in the neck! When will it be finished?

DADD: I really haven't the faintest idea.

(COLEMAN comes closer to plead.)

COLEMAN: *(Sighs.)* Look, I know 'e's only an amateur …

DADD: He barely knows which end to hold a paintbrush!

COLEMAN: E'll work 'ard to be better. 'E just wants to 'elp!

DADD: That's what the demon calling itself father used to say.

COLEMAN: *(Furious.)* Would be so much easier if your father were a monster, wouldn't it? Unfortunately, 'e was a good, kind man 'oo loved you. An' you murdered 'im.

(DADD ignores him and continues painting.)

DADD: I really can't use Dr. Minor.

(Pause. Without DADD seeing COLEMAN takes swig from hip flask, then gets out notebook and pencil.)

COLEMAN: So, it's like that, eh? Let's see then. Today's notes. For attention of Superintendent. 23rd July, patient quiet and co-operative in 'is room. 'Owever became very agitated and ramblin' into all sorts of weird talk while workin' on the curtain. Perhaps for 'is peace of mind … 'e needs a complete break from paintin'.

(COLEMAN and DADD glare angrily at each other.)

DADD: I have to work! I cannot stop!

COLEMAN: You 'elp me Mr. Dadd, and I can 'elp you. You *will* let Dr. Minor assist you. An' if you want to carry on paintin', I also need to talk to you about your father. We still need to understand why it 'appened.

(Lighting change, COLEMAN comes downstage and swigs from flask again.)

I said I was *tryin'* to stay off the drink, not succeeding. It was wrong to threaten 'im, but the alternative was to watch Dr. Minor go under. Anyway, without 'elp, this'll never be ready in time for the play! Wha's the time? *(Looks at Pocket Watch.)* August! By now, the situation with Christiana Edmunds was much worse. I was totally obsessed and she'd become the Venus of Broadmoor. But that's another story. And you've not come to 'ear about me. I've not murdered anyone! Yet. Oh, Chrissie …

(He steps aside. MINOR watches DADD work, trying to engage him in conversation. DADD ignores him.)

MINOR: I really am most grateful, Mr. Dadd.

I may not be of a standard for apprentice yet, but even assistant is an honour! I will watch most carefully, and learn!

Yes, Coleman just wants to speed up the work, but I understand that the act of creation cannot be rushed.

That sea is astounding. The way you make the surface glitter, but still catch the depths of water. Anything could be hiding there. What I would give to paint a sea like that!

I would have to learn the use of these fine detail brushes first I imagine. This one looks like a single hair …

(Makes to touch the brush lying on the table.)

DADD: Don't touch the brushes!

MINOR: Sorry!

I could make some tea?

DADD: *(Sighs. Sarcastic.)* So you're a theatre lover?

MINOR: I prefer the penny theatres.

DADD: Trashy melodrama?

MINOR: Respectable people think so.

DADD: I am told that those revolting places were staging the story of my sacrifice to Osiris within days of the event, as if it were some common murder.

MINOR: I'm sorry to hear that. But I find going into those dark boxes thrilling. Like doorways into other worlds.

DADD: Boxes? Doorways?

MINOR: Figures of speech.

DADD: You're lying!

MINOR: No!

DADD: Why were those penny theatres so thrilling?

MINOR: *(Sighs.)* If you must know, because it was easy to find whores there after the show. I'm sorry Mr. Dadd – I would like us to speak honestly, as if … we were friends.

DADD: I will try and imagine that.

(Pause.)

So, who did *you* kill?

MINOR: A furnace stoker called George Merrett. I shot him in error while the balance of my mind was disturbed. God forgive me! Nothing more terrible than to murder an innocent man!

DADD: I wouldn't know. The apothecary and amateur geologist was anything but innocent, although Coleman thinks he was and still doesn't *understand* why I did it.

MINOR: He must have been some kind of monster, to drive you to such a deed.

DADD: Being a demon was an advantage to him at the end. I don't think he felt my knife at all. Or the razor. You know, I think it was his birthday present finally drove me to do it!

MINOR: Birthday present?

DADD: *(Father's voice.)* 'One day *my boy*, they'll call you a great artist. Go! Create new worlds! Wonders and marvels! I give you this special box of birthday paints so I can play a small part in your fame.'

MINOR: The gift of a loving father, surely?

DADD: Aahhh, but I'd seen him mixing those *paints* the previous night in his pharmacy!

MINOR: Your father was an apothecary?

DADD: No, alchemist!

(Lighting change. MINOR freezes. Enter ARIEL.)

ARIEL: Day before your twelfth birthday, a fever, coming downstairs in the middle of the night, a light under the pharmacy door which is ajar, looking in … a stink of sulphur, walls covered in symbols …

DADD: Flasks of frozen colours, drained of light …

ARIEL: His fat, sweating face in the gaslight, shadows scuttling about in the corners of the room, creep back upstairs and never speak about it, or he'll eat your soul!

DADD: *(To ARIEL.)* How do you know all this?

ARIEL: I was there! It was the same night that your father imprisoned me! Because I tried to protect you … *(Starts to cry.)* He did confine me,

By help of his most potent ministers,

Into a cloven pine; within which rift

Imprison'd …

DADD: thou didst painfully remain

A dozen years.

ARIEL: Till you set me free! In Cobham Park.

(It seems they might kiss. Lighting change, ARIEL exits quickly.)

MINOR: Mr. Dadd?

DADD: I know what I saw that night. A poisoned gift from the demon calling itself father. You'll say that yours is different, I'm sure. But that's what all the others said. I'll not open any more of them. I've learnt my lesson.

MINOR: I understand. Perhaps in time.

DADD: Or perhaps not. But we do have all the time in the world, despite what Coleman thinks. You can make that tea now. Then I'll set you a long, difficult exercise on how to make a good sea.

(Lighting change. COLEMAN steps forward to talk with MINOR.)

COLEMAN: 'Ow'd it go?

MINOR: I felt like Dante, when Virgil took him by the hand! How wonderful to watch him at work! The concentration and discipline!

COLEMAN: Bloody mindedness, yeah!

MINOR: And the uplifting subject! That mountain soaring into the sky! The crowds pressing upwards to reach the temple!

COLEMAN: You'll soon be best of friends!

MINOR: We'll be … master and apprentice! *(Becomes tearful.)*

COLEMAN: There now, Dr. Minor!

MINOR: I came out of the theatre in a daze and sat for half
an hour just watching trees by the kitchen gardens.
Sunlight on leaves and the sky rolling away forever. I can't
remember seeing anything more beautiful. And I can look
forward to tomorrow! I felt confined here, but now I'm set
free!

COLEMAN: What's 'e got you workin' on then? Sea or sky?

MINOR: *(Laughs.)* Mr. Coleman! It was my first day! I mixed
some paints. And he has given me an exercise to improve
my technique.

COLEMAN: 'Ow long you gonna be doin' that!?

MINOR: Oh I don't know! But I want to be able to make a sea
like his, or a sky like the one I saw today. Mr. Dadd will
know when I am ready.

COLEMAN: Yeah, course 'e will. *(To audience.)* The best laid
plans, eh? Well at least the Doctor was 'appy! But when I
looked in after that, the work seemed to be goin' slower
than ever. The weeks went by an' it was *(Looks at Pocket
Watch.)* September! I was using every excuse I could to
go over to the Women's Block in the hope I might bump
into Christiana. I invited 'er to sit on the Social Committee
so that I 'ad a reason for meeting up regularly. I was
smuggling in clothes and makeup for 'er – which could
'ave cost me my job. And to cope with the stress of it all, I
was drinking like a fish. A bottle of mine was found in the
cloakroom. I received a final warning from the Super Dr.
Orange. Everything was getting a bit … fraught. But that's
another story. *(Swigs from hip flask.)* It was getting fraught
over at the drop curtain too.

(DADD painting curtain, MINOR washing brushes.)

DADD: I need more carmine.

MINOR: You have none left, Mr. Dadd.

DADD: Magenta will do then.

MINOR: You're out of that too. *(Beat.)* Although I think there's plenty of everything you need in the box.

DADD: Ask Mr. Coleman to order more carmine and magenta.

MINOR: *(Smiling to himself.)* I will. And sienna. I'm sure it won't take more than a few weeks.

DADD: I'll work on the sea this morning.

(Pause.)

MINOR: You did say that … sometime, I might work on the sea with you?

DADD: When you have completed the exercise to my satisfaction. Get me some lapis for the sea.

MINOR: There's not much lapis left either I'm afraid.

(DADD throws paintbrush and rag down in rage.)

DADD: How can I work under these conditions?

(DADD takes a swig of tea and spits it out.)

And the tea is cold!

MINOR: I'll make some more.

DADD: Don't bother!

MINOR: I should leave.

DADD: … I'd rather you stayed.

MINOR: Why!? You clearly find my company vexing! Why did you invite me here in the first place?

(Pause.)

DADD: *(Sighs.)* Because if I didn't, Coleman threatened to tell the doctors that painting made me mad.

MINOR: That's monstrous!

DADD: Isn't it?

MINOR: Why didn't you tell me?

DADD: I thought you were in league with him.

MINOR: My visits here are a pleasure. But I would not force my company on anyone! I'll go. And I'll tell Mr. Coleman that you begged me to stay, but I refused.

DADD: …. I have misjudged you. I'm sorry.

MINOR: It's Coleman who should apologise. To both of us. Have a good day Mr. Dadd. I hope work goes well.

DADD: Dr. Minor! Wait! *(Beat.)* Why should Coleman deprive you of a source of pleasure? You can stay.

MINOR: *(Beat.)* I'll stay on condition that you say if you cannot bear having a student any more.

DADD: Very well.

MINOR: And that you accept me as your true apprentice.

DADD: *(Points.)* I'll set aside this patch of sea for you to paint, when you complete the exercise satisfactorily.

MINOR: Good. Then we can have a new beginning. And I'll start by making some fresh tea!

DADD: No. You can start by fetching me the box.

MINOR: Are you sure?

DADD: We need carmine and magenta. And lapis for the sea. We can't wait three weeks.

(MINOR and COLEMAN freeze. ARIEL enters.)

ARIEL: Forgot your lesson so soon? *(Whispers.)* The Osiris Box!

DADD: He just wants to help.

ARIEL: And that's what the father demon used to say.

DADD: Perhaps he's not like the others.

ARIEL: Perhaps he's worse! Trying to get inside your head.

DADD: It's just paints! I need to work!

ARIEL: Your father gave you paints. Choose carefully.

DADD: Magenta and carmine. Lapis for the sea.

(DADD opens box. Lighting change to red. Everyone crowds round ominously.)

ARIEL: Poisoned gift.

MINOR: Greek gift.

COLEMAN: Egyptian gift.

DADD: What's happening?

ARIEL: You've lifted the lid. So now Mr. Coleman will want his *explanation.*

COLEMAN: *(Gets out notebook.)* Great that you and Dr. Minor are getting on so well and you've decided to use 'is paints after all, Mr. Dadd. Now that you're opening up a bit, it's time we talked about why you really did it! For the notes! Hieroglyphs in the sky over Karnak, you said, speakin' to you. What did Osiris say exactly?

(DADD pulls out large knife and cut-throat razor from box, arms across chest in Egyptian pose.)

DADD: I see myself in you and in you I am reborn. Open up. Let me in. You are my son.

COLEMAN: But you already 'ad a father! What did 'e 'ave to say about it?

(Lighting change. MINOR becomes DADD's father and they all act out the murder.)

MINOR: I blame your sunstroke in Egypt! You've been so disturbed since you got back. That's why I insisted on the visit to St. Luke's! Remember what the doctor there ordered? A total cessation of work!

DADD: Why are you trying to stop me working? What are you?

MINOR: Richard! You are my son!

DADD: Then, *father*, will you come on a special trip with me … to the countryside?

MINOR: Of course! I want to help. I've been worried sick about you for months. We can be alone together, just the two of us, a trip to re-establish the bonds of nature. Father and son.

DADD: To the countryside!

MINOR: Great restorer!

ARIEL / DADD: Let's go for a walk, father.

MINOR: We've travelled far enough today Richard. I'm tired and hungry. Let's eat and find somewhere in Cobham for the night. Remember the Ship Inn where we always used to stay? They'll look after us! Look! There's old John Adams, the waiter! John!

COLEMAN: Mr. Dadd! Good to see you! It's been a long time. Master Richard!

MINOR: Do you have a room for tonight?

COLEMAN: Sorry Mr. Dadd, we're full.

MINOR: Aahhh, I was afraid you might be!

COLEMAN: I could ask in the village. I'm sure we could find somewhere.

MINOR: Bless you John!

COLEMAN: Let me bring you some supper, then I'll go ask.

ARIEL / DADD: Let's go for a walk, father.

MINOR: John is bringing us supper now.

ARIEL / DADD: Afterwards!

MINOR: Afterwards we must settle into our room.

ARIEL / DADD: Later then!

MINOR: Don't agitate yourself boy! You know what the doctor said! Let's see what time it is when we've left the luggage in our room.

ARIEL: Supper is finished.

DADD: The luggage is in our rooms.

ARIEL / DADD: Let's go for a walk, father.

MINOR: I'm tired Richard. It was a big supper, and the porter and whisky have made me drowsy.

ARIEL / DADD: Just a short walk then.

MINOR: Might it help compose your mind for sleep?

DADD: It might help us both rest easier. Great restorer, you always say.

MINOR: All right. A very short walk.

DADD: To the countryside.

ARIEL: Where millions of spirits sleep invisible

On every leaf and blade of grass! All whispering!

ALL: *(Whisper.)* Richard!

DADD: To the Nile Delta.

COLEMAN: It was a short walk, you say.

ARIEL: Just out of sight.

DADD: Far enough away …

ARIEL: … from the lights of the village.

DADD: Into the growing darkness …

MINOR: … the park of Cobham Hall …

COLEMAN: Near the big chalk pit known as Paddock 'Ole …

ARIEL: Surrounded by lovely trees …

MINOR: Moonlight on the leaves, Richard! How beautiful!

DADD: Osiris said there would be a signal.

COLEMAN: An' was there was a signal?

ARIEL: He aped the god's words.

MINOR: I see my younger self in you, and your company makes me feel young again. Please don't shut me out Richard. You are my son. Let me in.

COLEMAN: This was the signal, you say, and as you walked side by side in Cobham Park, you were … impelled by a feelin' that some *sacrifice* was demanded by the gods, and spirits above.

DADD: The cutting of the wood …

(DADD and MINOR act out the murder. Nasty, brutal and physical.)

ARIEL: And I sprang upon the demon calling itself father and stabbed him in the left side …

COLEMAN: You attempted to slit 'is throat with the razor, failed, and then …

ARIEL: Finished him off with the knife.

(MINOR dies.)

COLEMAN: When your father fell, posin' yourself with upstretched arm, you thus apostrophised the starry bodies …

DADD: Go! And tell the great god Osiris that I have done the deed which is to set him free!

COLEMAN: Local people passing found the body face down on the ground next morning.

ARIEL: Near Paddock Hole thy father lies,
With bloody pearls that were his eyes:

COLEMAN: They called it Dadd's Hole, afterwards.

DADD: Art is about sacrifice.

COLEMAN: Pure bloody-mindedness!

DADD: *(Whispers.)* Father?

ARIEL: Osiris!

(Pause. Lighting change. Projections of the fairy feller. Green lighting. Noise of whirring crickets.)

DADD: *(Dazed.)* What place is this?

ARIEL: That sunless box you painted.

DADD: Frozen colours, drained of light …

ARIEL: Stalks of grass, towering like trees …

COLEMAN: Giant jungle leaves …

ARIEL: Fairies …

COLEMAN: Goblins …

ARIEL: A midget witch …

DADD: A crazy, cross-eyed elf.

COLEMAN: Apothecary …

DADD: No, alchemist!

COLEMAN: Knowin' they can't escape …

DADD: And strewn across the forest floor …

ARIEL: Acorns …

COLEMAN: 'Azelnuts …

DADD: A splatter of dark seed …

ARIEL: Like strange, ancient rocks …

COLEMAN: An' right in the middle …

ARIEL: With his back to you …

COLEMAN: An' 'is axe raised …

ARIEL: A woodcutter.

DADD: What's happening? Why am I back here again?

(Noise of crickets stops.)

ARIEL: You chose to use Dr. Minor's paints. Just as you used the paints your father bought you. Still not strong enough to refuse a poisoned gift. You've been using them for weeks and their poison is seeping into your bloodstream. Every day you use them, he grows more friendly and familiar. You let him in. It can't end well, but it has to end. You've always known that.

(ARIEL exits. Lighting change.)

COLEMAN: *(To audience.)* Alas, Dadd's dad was dead! I put it all in the notes, but there was still something missing. It was like I was finally startin' to make sense of the hieroglyphics on the tomb wall, and then the light failed. I asked him again why 'e did it. 'E just said it was unbearable to have a father like that. I gave up. What's the time? *(Looks at Pocket Watch.)* October! I couldn't spend any more time on Mr. Dadd because every spare minute I was making excuses to see Christiana. The Annual Ball was approaching, and she was desperate to go, but the Super thought it might get 'er over excited. I was feeling out of control, like I was about to do something stupid.

(Lighting change. MINOR gets up again and stands near the drop curtain. DADD enters this space with ARIEL hovering nearby.)

MINOR: A cold morning Richard! I banked the stove up high before you arrived, but it hasn't taken the chill off the room yet. Well, today is the great day!

DADD: Great day?

MINOR: My piece of the sea! You said yesterday that my last exercise was completed satisfactorily. I have mixed the lapis lazuli.

(Pause. DADD stares at ARIEL. She nods.)

Are you all right?

DADD: Dr. Minor. You cannot be my apprentice any longer.

MINOR: Richard … Mr. Dadd. I don't understand.

DADD: I don't need you to understand, only to accept the decision.

MINOR: But why?

DADD: Come, come!

MINOR: We talked about the importance of honesty. I want you to say it! Tell me why I cannot be your apprentice.

(Pause. DADD still watching ARIEL.)

DADD: Because your company has become … unbearable. And you have no real talent.

(Pause. MINOR examines his hands and arms.)

MINOR: I understand. It has *begun*. The monster must have started growing out. The markings will appear soon. I'll go.

DADD: Go. And take your box with you.

(MINOR goes over to box and wheels it away. COLEMAN swigs from hip flask.)

COLEMAN: The Annual Ball. Dr. Orange prevented Chrissie from going. She went 'ysterical, 'ad to be sedated and put in the Infirmary for the night.

(Waltz music. Red lighting. He takes another swig.)

I kept imaginin' 'er wakin', an' 'earin' the music through the walls, an' goin' mad with it. I couldn't bear it. Soon after the ball started, I crept away an' went into the

Infirmary. Christiana was the only woman in there that night. It was a crazy risk, goin' into the Women's section with no good reason, but I managed to duck into 'er room without being seen.

She was lyin' on top of the covers. *(Gulps from flask.)* There was one high, barred window and moonlight was streamin' through it across 'er bed. Red hot embers were still burning in the grate, and the room was close and warm and full of the gorgeous smell of her. I closed my eyes and breathed it in. I opened them again. My face was wet with tears. Funny, I couldn't remember crying. Chrissie …

(Music Stops.)

I opened Pandora's box that night. And if anyone ever finds out what 'appened, I'll lose my job. What's the time now? *(Looks at Pocket Watch.)* November! The first frost. Still no sign of The Broadmoor Players ever gettin' their theatre back. For God's sake, Mr. Dadd, 'ow much longer?

(DADD continues painting without looking up.)

DADD: I couldn't possibly say.

(COLEMAN examines the drop curtain.)

COLEMAN: *(Sighs. Beat.)* Hey – is that me!?

DADD: As Aesculapius, the god of medicine, ascending the mountain to the Temple of Fame. He tended the sick, as you do.

COLEMAN: Why, thank you Mr. Dadd! I always thought I'd die and be forgotten. Unless I murdered someone. Don't need to now, do I? Famous! Tha's a kind gesture.

DADD: Not really. I'm restricted for models here and I didn't want to base every famous person of antiquity on a homicidal lunatic.

COLEMAN: Is Dr. Minor not here today to help speed things up?

DADD: He left earlier. *(Sarcastic.)* I think the painting may have made him unwell.

COLEMAN: I'd not noticed 'e was unwell.

DADD: Oh yes. Became very agitated at times, rambling into weird talk.

COLEMAN: About what?

DADD: Egypt mostly. Even I tired of it, and I'm the son of Osiris!

COLEMAN: *(Coldly.)* Very good Mr. Dadd. Very funny.

DADD: I think he needed a complete break from painting.

COLEMAN: And you told 'im that, did you? Have you any idea what that will do to 'im!?

DADD: I know what it would do to me. That wasn't important to you back in July, was it?

COLEMAN: I'll go and find 'im and bring him here. You will apologise and ask him to come back and assist you, or so help me God, I'll …

DADD: What, kill me? Mr. Coleman, you look quite murderous! There's no need. Look, *(Points to drop curtain.)* You're already famous without going to all the trouble!

COLEMAN: God give me strength …

DADD: He will! But you have to open up first and let him in!

(COLEMAN exits. Lighting change. ARIEL enters clapping.)

ARIEL: Well done Richard! I kept you company while you learned your lesson. You've learnt it well. Now it's time to keep your part of the bargain. I have to go.

DADD: What? Must I be alone again?

ARIEL: Our revels now are ended. I'm Ariel, a free spirit! I can't stay in *Broadmoor*, can I? I want to go back – to light and air and clouds.

DADD: *(Tearful.)* Please don't leave me!

ARIEL: I can't leave you. You have to let me go. If you … love me enough.

(*DADD breaks down sobbing. ARIEL consoles him.*)

There now. Hush! It'll be all right. Open up. Let me in. Then let me go.

DADD: My brave spirit! Go.

(*Reluctantly, DADD kisses her goodbye. Stage flooded with red light. Loud, roaring noise of flames. DADD collapses as if poisoned by kiss.*)

You're not Ariel!

ARIEL: The gods love to play tricks!

DADD: You lied to me!

ARIEL: I did! What fun! Like a comedy about some idiot falling in love. I did say be careful who you trust!

DADD: Just like the others!

ARIEL: Much worse!

DADD: You weren't protecting me!

ARIEL: Your father was protecting you! He imprisoned me in the box, but you set me free! That was when I ate your soul.

DADD: Who are you?

ARIEL: My name is Legion, for we are many. Others will come after me, hiding inside patients, like Dr. Minor, and inside the attendants. You can trust no one.

(*COLEMAN enters wheeling the box.*)

COLEMAN: Would you like to take a look at your latest creation Mr. Dadd? This is how I found him. This is what you've done to him.

(He opens lid of box. Roaring of flames stops. MINOR stands up, and turns slowly round. He is covered in hieroglyphs. He holds an artist's palette and makes warpaint markings on his face, then takes dollop of paint onto his fingers and eats it.)

MINOR: Atum ate the dark seed of his loneliness, and he gave birth to demons and they grew out through his flesh. And they lived forever. I'd like to play a small part in your fame Mr. Dadd, but I cannot, because my company is unbearable and I have no real talent.

(Sucks paint off fingers and lets drop from his mouth onto palette. Mixes it all in with his fingers. Offers the paints to audience.)

(Whispers.) But still, look! I have mixed your paints!

(COLEMAN grabs shirt at DADD's throat.)

COLEMAN: Would you like to crack another fucking joke!? Are you happy now? With what you've done to Dr. Minor? What you did to your father? Why do you do these fucking things!?

DADD: Because it's unbearable!

COLEMAN: What's unbearable?

DADD / ARIEL: Love!

(COLEMAN lets go. DADD falls to his knees crying, mirrored by ARIEL.)

DADD: Can't you understand? It has made me mad!

(Pause.)

COLEMAN: I understand.

(COLEMAN embraces and comforts DADD. MINOR has noticed ARIEL. Echoing soundscape of whispers, fairy laughter, wind, running water and rain as at start.)

MINOR: Don't think I can't see you.

ARIEL: No one else sees me. Or hears me.

MINOR: I hear every word. But you're not like the others.

ARIEL: A demon? No. Don't you recognise me?

MINOR: I don't know.

ARIEL: You should. You created me. Out of light and air and clouds. To relieve your loneliness.

(Blackout. Sounds louder for a while, then silence.)

THE MURDER CLUB

'The Murder Club' is dedicated to
Olive Young (aka Gertrude Yates) (1897–1922)
and William Terriss (1847–97)

Characters

JOHN COLEMAN
Principal attendant, 'Gentlemen's Block',
Broadmoor

RICHARD PRINCE
Patient at Broadmoor 1897–1937. Failed actor,
conductor of Broadmoor orchestra

RONALD TRUE
Patient at Broadmoor 1922–51.
Affable, psychopathic conman with a
morphine habit

OLIVE YOUNG
Ghost of prostitute murdered by True

SET

Main acting area represents an empty cell at Broadmoor now used for meetings. There is a small table and three chairs. Up stage right is a music stand from which Prince conducts the orchestra. All of these are initially covered in dustsheets. There are a few other shapes under dustsheets as well which are never uncovered. These shapes are suggestive of furniture, or perhaps something more ominous. Preset on the table are a dictionary, notebook, pencil and newspaper. Front or side of stage is the corridor outside this cell. Coleman's stool in this corridor also. Olive's costume allows her to merge into the dustsheets whenever she wants.

HISTORICAL NOTE

On 16th December 1897, out of work and impoverished actor Richard Prince waited outside the Stage Door of the Adelphi Theatre in London. William Terriss, the most popular matinee idol of his day arrived with a friend soon after. Stepping from the shadows, Prince produced a dagger and in front of the witness, stabbed Terriss to death. Prince was convinced that Terriss was part of a conspiracy to keep him out of work. Ironically, it seems that he had actually been the beneficiary of Terriss' famous generosity towards struggling fellow actors. Prince was tried, found guilty but insane and sent to Broadmoor.

Ronald True thieved and lied his way through high society. He also conned his way into the Royal Flying Corps and several flying schools posing as an ace pilot even though he had crashed at least five aeroplanes. True blamed many of his crimes on a doppelganger whom he called 'the other True.' On Sunday 5th March, 1922, he stayed the night at the flat of a prostitute called Olive Young whom he had pursued obsessively for the previous fortnight. He killed her and stole valuables from her flat. He was soon picked up, charged and tried for murder. Like Prince he was found guilty but insane and sent to Broadmoor. After the verdict, he remarked to one of the warders 'I knew I should never be hanged. After all, I've committed no crime.'

'*The Murder Club*' is set in Broadmoor in 1922. It is the twenty-fifth year of Richard Prince's incarceration, and shortly after the admission of Ronald True.

SCENE ONE

(Preset. Low red lighting. Dustsheets cover most of stage. Loop of Elgar's 'chanson de matin' playing. Music fades. OLIVE comes forward.)

OLIVE: *(Whispers.)* Mother!

(Change to low white lighting.)

That's the most common last word of soldiers on the battlefield apparently. Natural I suppose, surrounded by fear and blood and death. But why was it my last word? I hated the stuck-up cow! We had our final falling out when I decided on a career change which would half my hours and double my wages. Oh, mother didn't mind me working twelve hours a day at the fur store, being goosed up by the manager every five minutes! But she wasn't happy with my new job where men paid for the privilege. 'You've destroyed my happiness, Gertrude! If your father finds out, it will kill him! If the neighbours find out, we'll have to move! At least do the right thing now! Don't ever show your face in this house again. Go now, and go quietly.'

Yes, mother loved melodrama! And murder mysteries. Her favorite actor was William Terriss. She'd see his shows over and over again. Had the hots for him I imagine. She loved romance! No, darlings, it don't run in the family. But the year I was born, Terriss was stabbed to death. 'I cried for days. The funeral route was lined with women crying. You could barely get into the cemetery! Proper man, he was my dear. Handsome, kind. Gave money to all the out of work actors, even the actor who killed him and do you know what Richard Prince did with that money? Went straight out and bought a knife to murder him with. I can't bear to watch murder mysteries any more!' Mother queued for hours to get into the trial so she could get a look at the murderer. They all hissed like it was the panto villain when he came into court. He loved that, apparently. Twenty years after Terriss died, mother was still going on about him! 'To think I actually saw him stabbed on stage!

Poor Mercutio! Such beautiful death scenes, Romeo and Juliet!' I got so sick of listening to her guff, one day I said, 'Bet the real thing weren't so pretty? That loony with the knife up a dirty alleyway?' She never mentioned his name again. I always thought there was too much prettifying of murder, even before I was done in. And if I'm ever going to understand why it happened, it's more important than ever to see things as they really are.

(Lights up on the cell. OLIVE pulls off a dustsheet to reveal COLEMAN and PRINCE seated at a table. She indicates them as she talks about them.)

Which is why I'm here! In Broadmoor Criminal Lunatic Asylum, with Richard Prince, and Mr. Coleman, principal attendant, Gentlemen's Block. Ronald True, the man who caved in my skull with a rolling pin will be along in a minute. Funny how things work out, isn't it?

SCENE TWO

(OLIVE moves to side of stage and merges into wall. The other two unfreeze. COLEMAN reading paper, PRINCE paces impatiently looking at pocket watch. COLEMAN doing his best to ignore questions.)

PRINCE: Is this the best they can do? Why can't we have the meeting room?

COLEMAN: Fully booked.

PRINCE: Do they value our work at all? And he's late! Who does he think he is? I have orchestra practice at eleven! Why does he have to be on the social committee anyway?

COLEMAN: The Super's decision. Get used to it.

PRINCE: You realise he's taken Jones on?

COLEMAN: I thought Jones was your man?

PRINCE: True is paying him more!

COLEMAN: You've lost a good 'un there.

PRINCE: And I will have to go back to *Simpson!* So unreliable!

COLEMAN: I don't think Mr. Simpson really wants to be your man again, Mr. Prince.

PRINCE: Well, there's no one else on the Block free! He'll have to do it until I can find someone better! I've already told him.

(COLEMAN sighs and returns to paper.)

I suppose you know True is an opium addict? He acquired the habit in Shanghai.

COLEMAN: That right?

PRINCE: Swanning round like he owns the place! His picture in the papers! Am I supposed to be impressed?

COLEMAN: *(Shakes head over newspaper.)* The mess in Mesopotamia! Liberate 'em from the Turks, and now they're shooting at our boys, and refusin' to pay taxes. Buggered if I understand any of it.

PRINCE: Are we here to discuss foreign affairs, Mr. Coleman?

COLEMAN: You should take an interest in the wider world.

PRINCE: If the bloody savages are mad enough to resist the benefits of British rule, then we should bomb them back to their senses! I would have thought that was *obvious!*

(Turns to racing pages of paper.)

COLEMAN: Hmmm. Unlike the 2.30 at Kempton, sadly.

(TRUE enters, laughing.)

TRUE: What ho! Sorry I'm a little late!

PRINCE: Exactly ten minutes late actually.

TRUE: Young Simpson buttonholed me. Wanted to know if he could be my houseboy! I told him I already had Jones, but he wouldn't take no for an answer and seemed quite upset. I had a cup of tea in his room with him to try and calm him down. Doesn't seem too well. In fact, given our location, I'd say he's probably off his chump! I say! Why all the shrouds? Have they put us in the mortuary? Just the ticket for a bunch of mad killers, what! Any stiffs tucked away?

(He peers beneath a few sheets.)

COLEMAN: Just an empty cell used for storage.

TRUE: You must be Mr. Prince.

(He holds out hand. PRINCE folds arms.)

COLEMAN: Now, now!

TRUE: Quite all right, Mr. Coleman. I have to earn Mr. Prince's respect. Jones says he hopes there are no hard feelings and that you'll remain friends.

(Gets out cigarette case.)

Do you mind?

PRINCE: Yes. It's a filthy habit.

COLEMAN: Mr. Prince!

(Dangerous pause. TRUE puts cigarettes away.)

TRUE: It can wait. Studying form for the big one at Kempton, Mr. Coleman. Little tip?

COLEMAN: Surely! Last three selections 'ave run like donkeys.

TRUE: Source in the stables. Normally excellent. Captain Cuttle's the nag. Put your shirt on the beast. You won't regret it.

(COLEMAN makes a note on his racing paper. TRUE stops short, winces and puts hand to his bad hip.)

COLEMAN: Captain Cuttle … You all right, Mr. True?

TRUE: Bit of German steel they never got out. Not a good night's sleep since I arrived.

COLEMAN: *(Beat.)* I don't think they'll let you 'ave any more morphine.

PRINCE: Ha!

TRUE: Doctors always think I'm pushing my luck, but normal doses just aren't effective any more. Don't worry. My own weakness to blame. And Shanghai!

COLEMAN: Sorry I can't do more Mr. True.

TRUE: Never mind, Mr. C. Oh, and please call me Ronald.

(Lighting change and others freeze. OLIVE steps forward.)

OLIVE: 'Ronald' and 'Mr. C' already. Fast worker. Blink and you'd miss him. Same with the other thing actually. The war wound?

(She slaps TRUE's backside as she walks past.)

Syphilis. I didn't live long enough to realise he'd given me a dose, but my poor friend Lizzie Wilson copped it off him. Asked me to call him Ronald on that first visit. Quite a charmer! And God, could he talk! The places he'd been to.

TRUE: In the mounted police in Canada!

OLIVE: Manager of a mine on the Gold Coast!

TRUE: Mexico, New Zealand, Argentina …

OLIVE: Charm faded when I realised he'd stolen five pounds from my purse before he left.

Richard Archer Prince. 'Actor,' inverted commas. He'll brag soon about the part he played opposite Henry Irving at the Adelphi. Mother was pleased as punch to have seen a real murderer on stage. 'He was 'second sergeant leading on the soldiers!' Truly awful! Only had two lines but missed his cue on the second one every night I saw it.

William Terriss was so … dashing as the lead! No wonder Prince hated him so much.'

Ronald's second visit was my last night on earth. He stood outside banging on the door for five minutes shouting …

TRUE: Olive! Let me in!

OLIVE: I still haven't worked out – after the purse business, why in God's name did I let you in a second time? Always prided myself on being a girl who could spot the nutters and say no. But you reminded me of someone I couldn't say no to, didn't you? Who was that, *Ronnie?*

TRUE: I warned you about using that name, Gertrude.

(Lighting change, others unfreeze. They act around OLIVE as if she is not there.)

COLEMAN: Welcome to the Social Committee, Ronald.

TRUE: So! There's to be an evening of entertainment!

COLEMAN: Mr. Prince – what musical delights are in store?

PRINCE: Our featured composer this year will be Sir Edward Elgar, and there are special reasons for the choice. Did you know, Mr. Coleman what Sir Edward Elgar's first job was?

COLEMAN: Can't say as I do.

PRINCE: Band conductor at the Worcester County Lunatic Asylum. This is Elgar's lesson! However humble the starting place, those who strive may achieve their dreams. The mightiest empire the world has ever known offers such opportunities to its citizens! I have written to Sir Edward care of Malvern Post Office inviting him to a concert of his music played here. I hope the idea might appeal to his charitable instincts.

COLEMAN: Lovely idea Mr. Prince! And what can you offer Ronald?

TRUE: A play of my own.

PRINCE: *(Sneers.)* Would we know it?

TRUE: New play, not quite finished, but I thought we could stage a few of the big scenes. It's called 'The Murder Club.'

COLEMAN: 'Oo are they then?

TRUE: Elite Gentlemen's Club – mysterious, shrouded in secrecy, pardon the pun. Cross between the Hellfire Club and the funny handshake brigade. But joining's not easy. First?

COLEMAN: Let me guess!

TRUE: Yes! You have to bump someone off! Nice part for you Mr. Prince, if you were interested?

PRINCE: Mr. True. I will be conducting the Broadmoor Orchestra as I have for the last twenty years.

COLEMAN: You could be missing a wonderful opportunity.

PRINCE: I have acted opposite Henry Irving at the Adelphi. I can live with the disappointment. I no longer act. I am a conductor.

COLEMAN: Which part did you 'ave Mr. Prince in mind for?

TRUE: Why, the hero of course!

PRINCE: *(Beat.)* What happens to him?

TRUE: I don't usually discuss unfinished work.

COLEMAN: Oh, go on Ronald!

(Pause. TRUE moves his chair closer to PRINCE.)

TRUE: *(Laughs.)* Oh, very well! Our hero is a struggling London actor! Kept out of work by one of the big stars. This man prevents him getting auditions, insults him, even mocks his poverty. One day, goaded beyond endurance, our hero kills his tormentor. He's facing the rope! But, superb actor that he is, he pretends to be bonkers! Stunt works and he's sent to …?

(Seeing impact of this on PRINCE, COLEMAN interrupts.)

COLEMAN: Ronald, I'm not sure …

TRUE: That's right! Broadmoor! Arrives and is settled in by the staff – small cameo for you Mr. C, but! Minor problem of getting out again! Bit stuck at this point. See, to get out, he has to convince them he's the full shilling after all, but then he'd swing. Any ideas?

(PRINCE is away, storming around room.)

PRINCE: I had the choice of killing him or starving! It was pure self defence! William Terriss would not rest till I was dead!

COLEMAN: Not again!

PRINCE: I only ask that people hear my side for once!

COLEMAN: We've 'eard your side over and over for bloody years, it's you 'oo never listens! You killed a good, kind man 'oo was loved by thousands. Left 'is poor wife and daughter heartbroken! And you've never so much as said sorry!

PRINCE: That's right! Paint me as the villain!

COLEMAN: You killed 'im! What do you want, a bleedin' medal!

PRINCE: There was provocation! Mitigating circumstances!

TRUE: Forgive me, Mr. Prince. I thought a melodrama based loosely on your case might tickle your fancy.

COLEMAN: It's a bit too ticklish for Mr. Prince.

TRUE: Never mind, I'll try to come up with a new idea.

(Pause. PRINCE gives COLEMAN withering look.)

PRINCE: No need. I'd be happy to read your script. If Mr. Coleman has no objection, of course?

COLEMAN: *(Sighs.)* Any other business?

PRINCE: Simpson. He's missed two orchestra rehearsals this week and is threatening to drop out.

TRUE: He was not a happy rabbit when I left him just now, poor man! I thought there was something on his mind.

COLEMAN: People can drop out if they want Mr. Prince.

PRINCE: Not from first violins! The strings in Elgar are crucial! He needs to realise how much good this will do him!

COLEMAN: *(Sighs.)* I'll pop up to 'is room now and talk to 'im.

PRINCE: I advise that you take a strong line!

COLEMAN: Excuse me a moment gentlemen. I'll leave you to chat a bit more about the play.

(COLEMAN exits. TRUE watches him go, then, unseen by PRINCE, he takes a swig from a small medicine bottle, closes eyes and breathes deeply. Lighting change, they freeze. OLIVE comes forward.)

OLIVE: The magic bottle. I'd almost forgotten. He'd barely set foot in my flat on that first visit and he was knocking it back. He asked me …

(TRUE unfreezes.)

TRUE: What's your poison?

OLIVE: I'm not sure you can afford that, dearie.

TRUE: Try a drop of mine.

OLIVE: What is it?

TRUE: Nectar of the gods! Do you a power of good!

(TRUE freezes again.)

OLIVE: I recognised the smell. What the hell, I thought. It'll help me sleepwalk through the business. And the peace afterwards … *(Closes eyes.)* Maybe *this* was the reason I let him in the second time. After he'd been banging on the door for five minutes, I went downstairs to him. *(Screams at him.)* Will you shut that bloody racket up!

(TRUE unfreezes. Grins and waves bottle at her.)

TRUE: Come to Wonderland with me, Alice!

OLIVE: It's Olive.

TRUE: I know that! Let me in, Olive. Pretty, pretty please?

(TRUE freezes. She takes bottle, addresses audience.)

OLIVE: And I did, because he reminded me of someone else. Just a spoonful and I was on cloud nine. He took a dose would knock out a horse and it just seemed to wake him up. He started jumping about, all excited.

(She gives bottle back. Lights change, others unfreeze. TRUE hurries across to PRINCE and talks excitedly, constantly watching over his shoulder for COLEMAN's reappearance.)

TRUE: Mr. Prince, we may not have much time! Please, listen! I must apologise to you again. I know all about your case! You're the reason I'm here!

PRINCE: I don't understand …

TRUE: The truth is beginning to come out about Terriss! How he schemed to destroy everyone who might be a threat to him! You have not been forgotten! You have friends determined to secure your liberty!

PRINCE: Who …?

TRUE: The Murder Club. We're real!

PRINCE: Real!?

TRUE: I'm your go-between. For now, we need to know only one thing. Are you determined to be free?

PRINCE: I …

TRUE: Permission to secure your liberty, old boy! Say the word, and it's done!

PRINCE: *(Beat.)* Yes!

TRUE: From now on, when I talk about the play, it may be a way to get information to you secretly from the Club. Comprende?

PRINCE: … I think so …Yes!

TRUE: The way Coleman spoke to you just now was a disgrace! He's no friend to your cause. He must know nothing!

PRINCE: Of course!

TRUE: So, no hint that we've had this chat. Stay frosty. Tick me off again! I'll pretend to lose my rag with you sometimes. When we're alone again, I'll tell you more.

PRINCE: I understand!

TRUE: We'll outfox him and the whole pack of them! We're actors, Richard!

(Puts hand out. This time, PRINCE grasps it firmly.)

PRINCE: Actors!

TRUE: Good man! Did you want Jones back by the way?

PRINCE: No, no! You keep him! I'll make do with Simpson.

TRUE: You're sure? Thanks! He is rather good.

(They separate as COLEMAN enters.)

You all right Mr C?

COLEMAN: Meeting's finished for today. We 'ave a serious situation upstairs with Mr. Simpson.

PRINCE: Creating a fuss over the concert? Oh for God's sake, he can go! I am tired of arguing with him!

COLEMAN: *(Shouts.)* You won't be arguing with 'im about anythin' any more! In fact if you so much as say another word to 'im …

TRUE: Oh dear. Is he all right?

COLEMAN: No, he's in quite a state. You were the last person to see 'im Mr. True, so Dr. Nicholson wants to talk to you in 'is office now.

TRUE: Of course.

(All three freeze. Lighting change. OLIVE wanders among them again.)

OLIVE: You've let him in now, haven't you, Mr. Prince? He called you 'Richard'. You're done for. Ronald has a thing about names. My trade name was Olive Young, but my real name was Gertrude Yates. Father's choice. Hard and ugly. Like him. When Ronald found out the name and how much I hated it, he was so chuffed. I begged him not to use it.

TRUE: I won't use it Olive, so long as you never, under any circumstances, call me *Ronnie.*

OLIVE: Course not Ronnie! When they told him his death sentence was commuted because he'd been judged insane, he said to a warder at Pentonville …

TRUE: I knew I should never be hanged. After all, I've committed no crime.

OLIVE: But months before he did it, he told Lizzie Wilson, just after he'd given her the clap …

TRUE: I'll kill somebody one of these days – you watch the papers and see if I don't. I'm perfectly certain I'll get off. I want to try it out.

OLIVE: Mad? Yes, so mad, he could lie his way into three pilot's jobs and crash five aeroplanes. Lie his way into every Hotel in London and leave without paying the bills. Fool a few doctors? No problem.

TRUE: There's another chap, spitting image of me and calling himself Ronald True! This blighter's going round London committing all these crimes and leaving the true True to take the rap!

OLIVE: This place! It's like the variety hall! He did it, but he didn't know what he was doing! He was so beside himself, he can't remember doing it! Someone else took him over and did it! He couldn't control himself! God told him to do it! The Devil! The Pope! King George! Uncle Tom Cobbley and all! I say, I say, I say! When is a murder not a murder? You tell me, darlings, you tell me. A judge, jury and doctors all bloody stupid enough to believe Ronald could be true? A man who lied his way round the world and conned almost every person he ever met out of money? Mad, darlings? My arse!

(Lighting change. Music. Truly awful strains of the Broadmoor orchestra's out of tune 'chanson de matin'. Exit PRINCE and OLIVE. TRUE and COLEMAN take seats at table.)

SCENE THREE

(As lights come up, COLEMAN is reading the paper. TRUE is wincing at the background music. After a while, the music stops.)

TRUE: Thank God! Do they improve with rehearsal?

COLEMAN: I think it makes 'em worse. Their first stab's often the best. Mr. Prince should be along in a minute. Very particular about timekeeping.

TRUE: Pity the same can't be said about his orchestra. How's Simpson today?

COLEMAN: No better. Never seen anyone go downhill so quickly. Like one of those poor lads went mad in the trenches. Gibbering and crying for 'is mother.

TRUE: *(Shakes head.)* A bad business. I was only with him ten minutes, but I keep asking myself if I said or did something that could have contributed to this.

COLEMAN: Mr. Simpson is very clear this is nothing to do with you Ronald, and Dr. Nicholson is satisfied. 'E's a quiet, 'armless soul 'oo's easy to bully. I've spoken my mind to Dr. Nicholson about the role of Mr. Prince. You know what he said about Iraq? 'Bomb the bloody savages back to their senses!'

TRUE: Upset you, hasn't it Mr. C? You're not yourself this morning. Look what you left by the kettle.

(He holds out COLEMAN's hip flask. COLEMAN takes it.)

COLEMAN: Was putting a drop in the tea, keep out the winter chill …

TRUE: Of course! And with all the pressure of your job, and this business with poor Simpson.

COLEMAN: *(Beat.)* Any'ow, what about Lord of Burghley?

TRUE: Not so sure this time. Bookies are like anglers. Stable lad gives out a few sound tips and that's their bait. Before you know it, they've reeled in the big money and we're all left looking like chumps. Tricky now that I can't actually look into the lad's eyes. Could always tell when the blighter was lying from his eyes.

COLEMAN: I can't see 'im getting another visitor's permit in the forseeable future.

TRUE: Course not.

COLEMAN: Very foolish thing to attempt, smugglin' that stuff in.

TRUE: Exactly what I said to him! 'Are you mad, boy?' Course, he thought he was being helpful! The whole business is such a damned shame. Because some nights here, not a wink of sleep … truly awful, Mr. C.

COLEMAN: *(Beat.)* Leave it with me. I can't promise, but I'll see what I can do.

TRUE: Bless you, old sport! No, I don't trust that lad any more! Hold back on Lord of Burghley.

(Enter PRINCE.)

PRINCE: Sorry I'm late, gentlemen.

COLEMAN: So what do you reckon about Iraq, Ronald? Mr Prince here reckons we should bomb them some more.

TRUE: Easy to say. I was in the Flying Corps. Know a bit about bombing. Out on the town a few weeks ago with one of the old squadron just back from bombing Kurdish villages in Iraq. Kendal. I'm having difficulty enough sleeping without the stories he told me. Our conduct in Iraq is a national scandal!

PRINCE: But it's war! You must have bombed the Germans!

TRUE: Spanking the Boche is one thing! But armoured cars against raggedy goatherds with Boer war rifles? Kendal dropped phosphorus fire bombs onto villages made of wood and reeds, full of women and children. Quite beautiful, he said. They make huge, white flares, dazzling even in desert sunlight, and water can't put them out. People ran from the villages on fire and were mown down by machine guns. He loved flying low to hear the screams and catch the stink of sulphur and burning. Great fun, he reckoned. Like flying over Hell, watching the punishment of the damned.

COLEMAN: Your Kendal is a disgrace to 'is uniform and 'is country!

TRUE: Decorated war hero obeying orders, Mr. C.

COLEMAN: So, we should bomb the savages, eh?

PRINCE: … I cannot believe his conduct is typical.

COLEMAN: Perhaps we'd better start the meetin'.

PRINCE: Yes, I need to get on. I have scheduled more rehearsal time later this morning. We are having to work extra hard to catch up now because of *Simpson.*

COLEMAN: *(Beat.)* You should show a little more respect, and think about your part in 'is situation.

PRINCE: How am I responsible!?

COLEMAN: Oh, not much! I told you, Mr. Simpson didn't want to be in your orchestra and 'e didn't want to be your houseboy! But would you listen?

PRINCE: Who is the wronged party here? Simpson has let down his colleagues in the orchestra! He has let me down personally! He has let down the whole of Broadmoor!

COLEMAN: I don't bloody believe it!

PRINCE: And I don't think that kind of language is acceptable in these meetings. I would like that minuted.

COLEMAN: *(Getting up.)* Stuff the bleedin' minutes! I'll just go an' tell Dr. Nicholson I think the concert needs to be cancelled this year because Mr. Prince isn't well enough.

PRINCE: That's not true!

TRUE: Gentlemen! Could we have a brief ciggy break? What do you think, Mr. Prince?

PRINCE: It might help.

COLEMAN: I'll take ten minutes with my crossword.

(COLEMAN exits and heads for corridor with his newspaper. PRINCE gazes angrily after him. TRUE takes a quick swig from medicine bottle and puts away again.)

PRINCE: Who does he think he's talking to?

(As he turns back, TRUE grabs him by the lapels. PRINCE cries out. Lights down on the two of them. They freeze.)

SCENE FOUR

(Lights up on corridor. COLEMAN settles down with newspaper. OLIVE walks around characters as she talks about them.)

OLIVE: Aaahh, the true True! That was the look in his eyes when he was on the job. Or later that night when he was killing me. Doing me, or doing me in. No real difference in Ronnie's eyes.

TRUE: I warned you about using that name, Gertrude.

OLIVE: He's not so unusual. I sometimes think there's just too many todgers in the world. Chopping them off at birth might be a bit disappointing for the men concerned, but there'd be less killing and wars, I'm sure of that. Even John Coleman here. His perfect ten minutes? Mug of tea with a large tot of brandy, and a juicy murder in the papers.

(COLEMAN checks round and then tops up tin mug from hip flask. Reads paper and drinks as OLIVE moves around addressing some lines directly into his face.)

Gets completely lost in all the lovely details. The newspaper said that Ronnie's murder weapon was a rolling pin, but it didn't tell you the best bits John. That I heard and felt my skull cracking. That when I opened my mouth to scream, I could feel bits of bone moving up there. Where bone isn't supposed to move. No scream, because he stuffed a towel in to keep the noise down. After that he could cheerfully bang away, like smashing open a pumpkin with a hammer. After my eyes filled with blood, I didn't see much more. But I was still alive. For quite a long time. Poor John. Deprived of all that vital information.

(COLEMAN opens dictionary and reads.)

When he's had enough war and murder, John likes to look up dirty words in the dictionary. What about 'Murder'? 'Noun. The unlawful, premeditated killing of a human being by another.' Not dirty enough for you John? What is it today then? *(Whispers, strokes his hair.)* Fellatio? Masturbation? Buggery?

(He sits back, closes eyes and whispers to himself.)

COLEMAN: Nipple!

OLIVE: Men never cease to surprise me.

SCENE FIVE

(Lights down on corridor. Lights up on cell. TRUE grips PRINCE tightly.)

TRUE: I'm working my socks off to secure your freedom and you're risking it all by loose talk about Simpson! They already think you pushed him over the edge!

(He lets PRINCE go. PRINCE backs away.)

PRINCE: I'm sorry. I am grateful for your efforts on my behalf. Have you … been in contact?

TRUE: All tickety-boo, don't worry! But nothing must prevent our evening taking place. There will be important people in our audience, watching you. They must be convinced on the little question of membership.

PRINCE: I have to murder someone!?

TRUE: Silly billy! You've already done that! No, you have to prove Terriss was a premeditated murder carried out when you were in your right mind.

(Pause.)

PRINCE: But my trial established I was not responsible for my actions! The balance of my mind was disturbed!

TRUE: Those arguments are for court where you have to prove you're barmy, old sport! They won't wash with the Murder Club! Do you want to rot in here for the rest of your days?

PRINCE: … Of course not.

(TRUE takes sheet of paper from his pocket and thrusts it at PRINCE. PRINCE hesitantly takes it.)

TRUE: Then learn this scene.

PRINCE: What's in it?

TRUE: A simple account of the facts and your state of mind at the time. You know, 'here's why and how I killed him, this is how he died.' This scene will convince our friends in the audience that you're sane and ready to be sprung. *(Beat.)* What's the matter?

PRINCE: I do not consider myself an evil man …

TRUE: *(Laughs.)* This has nothing to do with good or evil, old boy! Sometimes certain people have to die. If every individual murder had to be pored over first by lawyers, nothing would ever get done! When Mr. Churchill decides that a certain number of Kurds in Iraq need to be gassed, we trust his judgement.

PRINCE: Churchill is a member!?

TRUE: Rule Number One – never disclose a fellow member's identity! But it's not that hard to work out who we are, is it? Of course, we have to weed out loonies. Loonies who run round killing at random would bring the Club into disrepute!

PRINCE: Mr. True. These important people in our audience. They wouldn't include … Elgar?

TRUE: Not replied to your letter yet?

PRINCE: I'm afraid not.

TRUE: Not a Club member that I'm aware of. Unless you know something I don't? I know his wife died recently …

PRINCE: No, no, I wasn't suggesting anything like that! I just wondered if you knew whether he might be coming.

TRUE: Why is it so important?

PRINCE: We've been working on 'Nimrod' from the 'Enigma Variations.' My heart swells to bursting sometimes with the power of the piece! I can hear all the beauty and terrible sadness of the world, the solemn mystery of life and death. Eternal truth. To play it is like an act of prayer. Mr. True, you'll probably think me a little mad, but I would rather shake the hand of the man who wrote that music than gain my freedom.

TRUE: Richard! I had no idea the thing was so important to you! I'll have one of the Club pop round and talk to him.

PRINCE: You can secure his attendance?

TRUE: Our members sign bits of paper and thousands are blown to pieces in Iraq. Or millions starve in India. Hardly a problem to arrange the attendance of Sir Edward at the Broadmoor Glee Club!

PRINCE: Oh, Mr. True!

TRUE: But from now on, no more arguments with Coleman.

PRINCE: What shall I do if he keeps bringing up Simpson?

TRUE: Ignore him! He only does it to try and make you feel guilty! Like when he brings up Terriss.

PRINCE: That's true! I'll ignore him!

TRUE: Here he comes. Mother's the word!

PRINCE: Mother?

TRUE: Mum!

PRINCE: Of course! Mum!

TRUE: We're actors, remember?

PRINCE: Actors!

(COLEMAN enters. Lighting change, three men freeze.)

SCENE SIX

(OLIVE wanders among the others as she speaks.)

OLIVE: Takes two to tango, as we say in my trade. There's the murderer … *(She pinches PRINCE's cheek.)* 'Who's an ugly boy, then?' And the *murderee*. There's a new one for your crossword, John. My word. I was no one's bloody victim.

(She walks round set, addresses TRUE up close.)

But murder bound us together very deeply. True love. Born out of fear, blood and pain, splintered bone and splattered brains … Looking into the eyes of the person murdering you is a bit like looking into the eyes of God. The last thing I saw, through the blood in my own eyes, was the pupils of these eyes here opening up, wider and darker into a night sky. And it was full of stars. Right at the very end, no fear. Just peace. A perfect moment. Being murdered seemed the most natural thing in the world. And so much easier than all those years of father threatening to kill me, when the fear never ended.

And where were you all those years, mother? Out at the theatre maybe, weeping over some lovely death scene. So why were you the last word on my lips? Why would I call on you, of all people? A bloody ghost in your own house. Just like I am now. Nowhere to be seen.

SCENE SEVEN

(COLEMAN is outside alone in corridor pouring brandy into his tea from hip flask and drinking. TRUE sits looking bored and prompts from script as PRINCE paces about and stumbles over lines.)

PRINCE: And that is why, ladies and gentlemen, I say to you …

TRUE: I submit to you that in truth, I am innocent …

PRINCE: … innocent of any crime! The man I killed was a black-hearted villain, a villain …?

TRUE: Whose passing none should …

PRINCE: Lament! Furthermore, I was not mad when I did the deed. Oh no! Posterity? Posterity will be kind to me?

TRUE: You still don't know the lines!

PRINCE: I may have paraphrased a little. I'm sorry.

TRUE: I think we'll just improvise the next scene, shall we?

PRINCE: There's another scene?

TRUE: Well of course! The bloody murder scene! You have to show our guests how Terriss died.

PRINCE: Is that such a good idea?

TRUE: Oh for God's sake, man! You had the nerve to stab him! You must have the nerve to act it out! You're trying to persuade the Murder Club you're a cold-blooded killer who watched your victim die! If you can't pull this scene off, there's absolutely no point in inviting them in.

PRINCE: *(Beat.)* I can do it.

TRUE: Good.

(COLEMAN comes to cell door, pausing to take a swig from hip flask and then entering.)

Aahhh, Mr. C! Just in time. You can help us out in this scene. How would you like to murder Mr. Prince here?

COLEMAN: I've just come from seeing Mr. Simpson 'oo is worse than ever, so that sounds like a great idea.

PRINCE: I thought I had to be the murderer?

TRUE: Why should you have all the fun Richard? I think Mr. C might have more of the stomach for your part today. Let's imagine this pen is his knife. This is the alley where the deed was done. It was an alley, wasn't it Richard? Away from the street light, eh? Nice and dark. Victim by the stage door, key ready to open it.

COLEMAN: John Coleman's watching you from the shadows.

(TRUE hands COLEMAN pen, starts positioning PRINCE with his back to COLEMAN and with his hand up as if about to turn a key in a door.)

TRUE: Lovely Mr. C. Where was Graves standing Richard?

PRINCE: Who?

TRUE: Oh come on, you know damn well who! John Graves! Terriss' friend! The man who saw you do it! The man who held you and shouted for help until the police arrived! Main witness at your trial, remember? Where was he standing?

(PRINCE points to spot beside him. TRUE stands there.)

Thank you. Now where did you stab him first?

(Pause. PRINCE reaches over his shoulder and touches a spot between his shoulder blades.)

Mr. C?

(COLEMAN rushes across with a great roar and makes as if to stab, pausing the blade an inch from PRINCE's back. PRINCE reacts as if stabbed.)

COLEMAN: Aaaarrrggghhh!

PRINCE: Oh!

TRUE: And again. Twice in the back, wasn't it Richard?

(Pause. PRINCE says nothing.)

Go on.

COLEMAN: Aarrgghh!

(COLEMAN stabs again. PRINCE turns to face him, lifting arm to fend off further blows.)

PRINCE: *(Whispers.)* … My God!

TRUE: Good! Good! Keep it up! So he turned around, eh? Then you stabbed him again. Where this time?

(PRINCE points to his heart.)

Right in the heart? Lovely! Mr. C?

(COLEMAN brings the knife down again with another roar, stopping an inch from PRINCE.)

PRINCE: My God, I've … been stabbed!

TRUE: Look into his eyes, Richard. The man who's killing you. The last thing you're going to see on this earth.

(PRINCE slides slowly to the floor, staring into COLEMAN's eyes with a look of horror. TRUE kneels.)

Graves knelt briefly didn't he, to comfort his friend? Poor Terriss, bleeding his life out onto the London cobblestones. But then he was up and furious, to collar the murderer.

(TRUE gets up, and grabs COLEMAN's arm.)

(Shouts.) Murder! Police!

COLEMAN: Ronald! Keep your voice down!

TRUE: *(Roars.) Police! Murder!*

(Twists his grip on COLEMAN into an arm lock.)

COLEMAN: Steady on … You're hurting my arm!

(TRUE suddenly lets go and switches charm back on.)

TRUE: I'm sorry Mr. C! Quite carried away there! Didn't want to let the murderer escape!

(Offers PRINCE a hand and helps him up. COLEMAN straightens clothing.)

COLEMAN: All that racket will 'ave the riot squad on their way! I'll go and tell 'em no one's actually bein' murdered. Just sit quiet for a few minutes.

TRUE: We promise not to murder anyone, don't we, Richard?

(COLEMAN exits, OLIVE comes to life, others freeze.)

OLIVE: He actually said that to me at the door that Sunday night.

TRUE: Oh, let me in Olive! I promise not to murder you!

OLIVE: Everything was telling me, don't! So what the bloody hell was I thinking of?

(TRUE flashes a smile, and in her father's voice …)

TRUE: Gertrude?

OLIVE: Of course! *(Child's voice.)* Daddy?

TRUE: Open up please. Let me in.

OLIVE: I'm doing a poo.

TRUE: You have to come out eventually. You need to eat.

OLIVE: I'm not hungry.

TRUE: Unlock the door, Gertrude.

OLIVE: I'm frightened, daddy.

TRUE: There's no need. This time will be different.

OLIVE: He wasn't lying for once. That time was different. And all the times afterwards. As he hauled me screaming out of the bathroom and into his room, I caught sight of my mother sitting on the bed in her room with her fingers jammed into her ears. For years afterwards I just wanted to kill both of them. You and me aren't so different in some ways, are we Ronnie?

TRUE: I warned you about using that name, Gertrude.

(Lighting change. Others unfreeze.)

SCENE EIGHT

(As soon as COLEMAN exits, he takes hip flask out for a swig while TRUE takes medicine bottle from his pocket for a swig also.)

PRINCE: Is that how it must be on the night?

TRUE: Yes, do it big! Like Coleman! What's wrong with a bit of melodrama? Devils and gods! This isn't some filthy little tart being done away in a basement flat, is it? This was the murder of one of the greatest actors of our time! Why Kendal himself would have been proud!

(PRINCE staggers and sits down.)

You all right?

PRINCE: But Kendal kills casually, as if it were sport! Incinerating women and children! You made him sound like a monster!

TRUE: All that was only for Coleman's benefit! Kendal's a good egg! And a loyal Club member who does his job! Probably enjoys killing no more than you or I.

PRINCE: Mr. True, this has … taken a toll on me.

TRUE: A toll, Richard?

PRINCE: After twenty-five years, I had begun to put it behind me. But just now, enacting that scene, I seemed to feel what Terriss felt. The agony of that knife entering my heart. Blood filling my lungs! I couldn't breathe! I have never known such fear! What it is to die. And to be murdered. My thoughts are full of blood and fear and death.

TRUE: Richard, this sometimes happens in our line of business. You must be strong. Think of Elgar! Think of England!

PRINCE: I'm afraid!

(PRINCE sobs. TRUE comforts him.)

TRUE: There, there! Well, if a mere rehearsal reduces you to a gibbering wreck, maybe you should just do the confession.

PRINCE: Confession?

TRUE: Guess what? The whole play idea was really just for fun!

PRINCE: Fun!?

TRUE: Strictly speaking, a signed confession to murder for Club records is all you need to join.

(TRUE gets out a notebook from pocket and hands it to PRINCE.)

I did take the liberty of drafting one just in case. Based on your own words and what I've heard. Let me hear you read it through.

PRINCE: 'I Richard Archer Prince, being of sound mind, do hereby confess that I murdered William Terriss on 16th December 1897. I murdered him because he was rich, popular, successful, good-looking, generous and a talented actor. All this made me hate him more than any man alive.' What does this mean?

TRUE: Finish reading.

PRINCE: 'The more I dwelt on these things, the more aware I became of my own failure and inadequacy. I finally perceived that the only thing that could bring me any relief was killing him. So I did. And I have never regretted it.' I never said any of this!

TRUE: 'I may have paraphrased a little.'

PRINCE: These aren't my words!

TRUE: *(Sighs.)* Did he deserve to die?

PRINCE: Yes!

TRUE: Do you regret it?

PRINCE: No.

TRUE: Are you mad?

PRINCE: No!

TRUE: Bingo! Then it's murder! Copy it out.

PRINCE: What!

TRUE: A fair copy in your own hand. That's how it works. Club rules.

(Reluctantly, PRINCE begins to copy out the statement. He continues doing this on and off during the following exchanges. As he does so, TRUE takes another swig from his medicine bottle.)

That's it. What are words anyway? Let lawyers and psychiatrists and bloody politicians quibble about them. What the blazes would they know, eh? I knew you belonged in the Club the moment I set eyes on you. Anyway, if you're squeamish, remember, you only have to sign one of these.

PRINCE: What do you mean?

TRUE: Any more that you kill you're not required to sign for. Your membership's secure.

PRINCE: I wasn't planning to kill any more!

TRUE: Oh, you say that now, you don't know how you're going to feel after a year or two on the outside!

(He laughs. Pause. PRINCE finishes writing and slowly hands notebook over. TRUE glances at it and hands notebook back.)

Not signed. *(Beat.)* Well, it's not a lot of bloody use without your signature old sport, is it?

Come on Richard, just a formality. Coleman will be back soon. Be a good boy. Do you want your freedom? Do you want to shake the hand of Sir Edward Elgar?

(PRINCE slowly takes notebook and signs and hands book and pencil back to TRUE whose demeanour completely changes.)

PRINCE: How long will it take to get out?

TRUE: You're not going anywhere. Dangerous, self-confessed murderer like you? They'd be mad to let you out, Dick. Mind if I call you Dick?

PRINCE: What is this?

TRUE: There's no Murder Club, Dick. There's not even a play. I haven't written one.

PRINCE: My God!

(TRUE taps the notebook and lights a cigarette. He crosses stage and stands behind PRINCE. As he talks he blows smoke into PRINCE's face, runs finger inside his collar, etc. PRINCE flinches, paralysed.)

TRUE: Yes! Are you sweating, Dickie? Filthy habit, sweating. I thought about killing you when you stopped me smoking that first day. 'In here for being mad and killing anyway,' I thought, 'what could they do to me? Very little I suspect.' But then I realised I didn't need to kill you because you're already dead, Dickie. Oh, you'll carry on for another twenty years, pissing, shitting, waggling a stick at that bunch of cloth-eared morons you call an orchestra, but that's not life. You're so dead, I can smell the decay. I can almost see the maggots. There'd be no credit in killing someone like you, old boy, see? No, I'm going to let you live. That's my punishment.

(Pats his pocket with the notebook in it. He moves closer and closer to PRINCE as he continues.)

Any nonsense and we'll see what Dr. Nicholson makes of this. Maybe they'll decide you should swing after all. Imagine that! What a lark! As far as you're concerned, from now on, I'm a Horseman of the Apocalypse, Dickie. I'm your one True God. I'm the fucking Angel of Death.

(He kisses PRINCE on the lips. Enter COLEMAN. TRUE moves away.)

Mr. C! Hope we didn't create an international incident for you out there.

COLEMAN: You created a lot of problems for me actually Ronald. I met the riot squad piling down the corridor and I've just 'ad a very difficult time tryin' to explain to Dr. Nicholson what 'appened.

TRUE: I'm sorry, Mr. C. I really am. What happened was not good, but it's given me and Richard the chance to have a heart to heart. We've come to a decision.

COLEMAN: Oh? And what's that?

TRUE: This play is stirring up things that are better left dead and buried. After all, we're ill! And we came here to get better! Morbid thoughts don't help! Look at the way I started behaving towards you just now! Plays have this funny way of getting inside your head. Raising up demons. We're going to cancel it.

COLEMAN: That's a shame.

TRUE: But we've had a great idea for the future of entertainments here. Do you want to say, Richard, or shall I?

PRINCE: You.

TRUE: We're going to promote Sports Days. Richard is worried about people smoking because it's such a filthy habit and bad for their health. Fresh air, running about in the open, showing off a bit of flesh. What do you think, Mr. C?

COLEMAN: Dr. Nicholson'll love that.

TRUE: I want a challenge Mr. C, I think this might be it.

(TRUE checks his watch.)

Golly, we're keeping you from orchestra rehearsals, Richard. Run along now. Don't keep Elgar waiting!

(Broken, desperate glance and PRINCE exits.)

Narrow escape there, Mr. C!

COLEMAN: Oh?

TRUE: Dickie Boy! Coming out with all that *stuff* while you were gone. Deary me! There's a real Murder Club and he's going to join and they would ensure his release now that he was sane again! Better knock this on the head, I thought!

COLEMAN: Sounds like you did the right thing cancelling. A shame though. I was looking forward to it.

TRUE: It is a shame. I even think it was helping Dickie understand what he'd done and how poor Terriss suffered. Even beginning to feel remorse for his crime. Still, can't be helped. Unfortunately, once I'd got him off the idea of the play, he got on to the subject of rumpy pumpy. The human mind can be a filthy thing, John. I simply could not repeat some of the things he said.

COLEMAN: What things?

TRUE: Oh, the usual, you know. Tarts mostly. And queers.

COLEMAN: Queers!

TRUE: You know, I wonder whether anything went on, in that way, between Prince and Simpson.

COLEMAN: No!

TRUE: Handsome young lad like Simpson, older man … Might only take ten minutes. Alone in a room together for a cup of tea, and before Simpson knew it … What chance would the poor boy have? And that sort of thing could push a chap over the edge!

COLEMAN: I should 'ave bloody known!

TRUE: But we shouldn't jump to conclusions.

(COLEMAN pacing, agitated.)

COLEMAN: Bloody Richard Prince! Simpson is the quietest, nicest patient on the block! Just a kid.

TRUE: Mr. Coleman, for goodness sake, have a drink! *(Beat.)* I can see the hip flask. Go on, you've earned it! Was Simpson much worse today?

(COLEMAN takes a swig from hip flask.)

COLEMAN: Smashing his head against the wall, smearing blood and shit everywhere. The pity of it Ronald, it's almost unbearable. And do you know what's arrived for Mr. Prince today, of all days?

(He gets a letter out from his pocket.)

Came in the second post. Postmarked 'Malvern'.

TRUE: Oh my giddy aunt! Open it.

COLEMAN: What?

TRUE: With him in this state, you need to know what's in that letter before you give it to him.

(COLEMAN opens the letter and reads.)

COLEMAN: Blow me! Sir Edward's only accepted the invitation! *(Laughs.)* 'I would be able to relive the 'appy memories of a youth spent in Worcester Lunatic Asylum!' 'Ere's a turn up for the books! What's the matter?

TRUE: I'm not a doctor, Mr. C, but I would say that the last thing Dickie boy needs at the moment is any more excitement. I mean! Tarts. Queers. And now Sir Edward Elgar!

COLEMAN: You're right. Doesn't deserve it anyway. I'll get Dr. Nicholson to write back and put 'im off.

(Takes another swig from hip flask.)

And I'm glad 'e's not gonna be in your play! Swanning round like he owns the place! Stuff him! My mother took me to see William Terriss on stage you know.

TRUE: Really? Was he as good as they say?

COLEMAN: Unbelievable! So natural, it wasn't like watching a play at all! I came out of the theatre that night and told my mother I wanted to be an actor.

TRUE: And did you try?

COLEMAN: I was just a kid! Got a part in the Nativity play at school. What I remember most about it was looking out into the audience and seeing my mother watching me and smiling. She was so proud!

(He looks into OLIVE's eyes without seeing her.)

TRUE: Your mother? Bless her! Not with us any longer?

COLEMAN: No …

TRUE: What part did you play?

COLEMAN: Shepherd …

TRUE: And a good shepherd you still are, to your Broadmoor flock. Your mother would be proud of you all over again.

(He hands COLEMAN a handkerchief to blow his nose.)

COLEMAN: … most unprofessional.

TRUE: You know Mr. C, we don't have to cancel the play just because Dickie can't hack it. We could recast.

COLEMAN: *(Beat.)* Me!? Seriously?

TRUE: Your performance tonight as the murderer was far more convincing than anything Mr. Prince has been able to manage.

COLEMAN: Well I'd love to 'ave a go, thank you Ronald!

(TRUE winces and rubs leg.)

Are you all right?

TRUE: It's nothing.

COLEMAN: *(Beat.)* I've 'ad a word with a friend of mine. From Monday, I can get you a small amount each week if your mother agrees to send the money like you said.

TRUE: I'm at a loss for words. *(Tearful.)* You don't know what it means Mr. C just to be believed. To be trusted!

COLEMAN: There now!

TRUE: I've just been so upset lately. Not myself.

COLEMAN: You take this Iraq business to 'eart, don't yer?

TRUE: I can't stand bullying, I really can't. And that's what's going on over there! Keeps me awake, what Kendal said about that shepherd.

COLEMAN: What shepherd?

TRUE: They dropped delayed action bombs to catch the tribesmen tending their animals at night. Kendal went back with a foot patrol the next day and they found this old Arab shepherd. One of his legs blown off and half his guts spilling down the hillside. No one understood what he was groaning till the translator said he was asking them to kill him. Kendal refused of course. Said he might be needed for questioning, so they hauled him off down the hillside squealing like a stuck pig and Kendal enjoying every bump along the way. Stuffed a towel in his mouth when it got too noisy.

COLEMAN: That's disgustin'!

TRUE: Isn't it? They gas civilians and blow children to bits with their clever dick delayed action bombs and I'm supposed to break my heart about some poxy tart off the Finborough Road? What do they think, eh? And the men who give them orders? When they're *doing* it? *Bloody savages!*

COLEMAN: Easy, Ronald!

TRUE: Sorry. It's just so damnably unfair!

COLEMAN: What about this play then? Something to cheer us up! When can I start?

TRUE: Why not right away! Here's some lines for you to look at. We'll soon make a real murderer of you, eh Johnnie?

(They freeze. OLIVE unfreezes.)

OLIVE: 'Johnnie' now. So you've let him in too.

(PRINCE enters slowly, and goes to music stand to conduct. Addresses audience / orchestra.)

PRINCE: Gentlemen. Let us play.

(He starts conducting a hideous version of 'Nimrod' from the Enigma variations starts up.)

OLIVE: Not one of us can say no to you, can we? We've all let you in. How mad are we, *Ronnie?*

TRUE: I warned you about using that name, Gertrude.

OLIVE: I'm sick of hearing about good old Churchill bombing and gassing the Kurds. Those are real people you're talking about *Ronnie*!

TRUE: Stop it! It's horrible!

OLIVE: What about the horrible things you said? Racking their chests to breathe and lungs full of blood! Arms and legs blown off! Burning to death in a fire that water won't put out! That's not just in some play! They're real people, Ronnie!

TRUE: That's the last time you'll use that bloody name, Gertrude.

OLIVE: And it was. And then I had a real death too. One they wouldn't put on your bloody stage, mother. So different there, isn't it? Gentle music playing in the background. Lights dimming slowly and beautifully as I whisper 'I die, I die!'

(Lights dim slowly and beautifully. 'Nimrod' slides into beautiful version. Music swells slowly during speech. Low red lighting as at start.)

Nice little pause for the ladies to get out their fucking handkerchiefs. No place for me on your stage is there, mother? With my brains hanging out of my head, shitting myself, and a towel stuffed down my throat to stop me screaming. Where can I go then? 'If your father finds out, it will kill him! Go away! Don't ever show your face in this house again. Go now, and go quietly.' You think I'll go quietly? After what happened to me? You want to write me out of the script? Kill me off and you think I won't scream the bloody house down? Don't turn that music up! Don't! Take your fingers out of your ears, you stupid bitch!

Mother!

(Music cuts abruptly. Blackout.)

WILDERNESS

Another way
My sage guide leads me, from that air serene,
Into a climate ever vex'd with storms
And to a part I come, where no light shines.
Canto IV, Dante's 'Inferno'

'Wilderness' is dedicated to George Merrett, furnace stoker at the Red Lion Brewery (?–1872)

Characters

DR. WILLIAM CHESTER MINOR
Patient at Broadmoor Hospital,
1872–1910. Former surgeon.

MR. COLEMAN
Principal attendant, Block 2,
Broadmoor Hospital.

GEORGE MERRETT
A ghost. Furnace Stoker, murdered by Minor.

ELIZA MERRETT
His wife.

SET

Main acting area represents a composite of Minor's two rooms at Broadmoor. The back room is his library and study. This may be represented stylistically – e.g. books dangling from ceiling by wires or coming out of the wall at odd angles, words and definitions painted in large typeface on the walls, etc. There is also a desk or bureau piled with books and papers, two decanters and glasses. The larger front room is Minor's bedroom and parlour. There is something to represent a coal fire, perhaps with a hearth. There is also a camp bed to one side. Front or side of stage is the corridor outside Minor's cell where Coleman spends much of his time. Coleman's chair is in the corridor.

HISTORICAL NOTE

William Chester Minor (1834–1920) was a surgeon in the U.S. Union Army during the American Civil War. Terrible experiences there weakened an already fragile mind and the Army pensioned him off. He came to live in London where he walked out of his lodgings in Lambeth on 17th February 1872 and shot a complete stranger dead. The man was George Merrett, a furnace stoker at the local brewery. Minor was imprisoned in Broadmoor for the next thirty-eight years where he became deeply involved in the writing of the Oxford English Dictionary. Eliza, the widow of his murder victim, visited him for a number of years and, although illiterate herself, brought him books from London for his Dictionary work.

SCENE ONE

(Preset; dim red lighting. MINOR sleeping in his cell. Music playing. Attendant COLEMAN sits in corridor outside cell, reading penny dreadful. Lights down to black. Fx of artillery shelling starts and builds slowly. Dim red lights up again on MINOR's cell. Shelling louder. MINOR leaps from bed and rushes to cell door.)

(Shouts.) Mr. Coleman! They're coming for me! Mr. Coleman!

(Shelling fx ceases abruptly. Snap to black. Lights up on COLEMAN in corridor with his hip flask and penny dreadful which he holds up.)

COLEMAN: At the end of a night shift, a little distraction helps keep you awake. 'The Monkey Boy of Madagascar – infant suckled by apes on island paradise!' I know it's rubbish, but we all love a good monster.

(Lights up on cell, MINOR sits up in bed and goes through his morning ritual, which continues as COLEMAN speaks. Spits onto floor, scrapes tongue with fingers, paces cautiously around cell looking under bed and desk, behind furniture etc.)

1872. Richard Dadd painted the Broadmoor theatre and I fell in love with the Chocolate Cream Poisoner and fell off the wagon. Cheers! *(Drinks.)* ... and patient number 742 was admitted. It's all in 'ere, but this cheap, nasty print gets your fingers all grubby. If I tell you the story though, you can keep your 'ands clean. Anyway, the penny dreadfuls sometimes miss the best bits out, and what use is that? Like a dictionary without the dirty words!

(Puts magazine down, wipes hands, indicates cell.)

The criminally insane do give Broadmoor a bad name, but for thirty-eight years, we could point to 'im and say Dr. William Chester Minor! A bit of a genius, and 'elping to write the Oxford English Dictionary!' The editor Dr. Murray wrote to 'im ...

MINOR: 'So enormous have been your contributions, we could easily illustrate the last four centuries from your quotations alone!'

COLEMAN: All right, 'e also murdered a bloke, but 'e apologised! Anyhow, when 'e was a surgeon in the American Civil War, 'ow many lives did 'e save, eh? It's all of a man's life that counts.

Lucky for 'im the dictionary work came along. You need a lot of distraction for thirty-eight years in Broadmoor.

MINOR: Imagine ...

COLEMAN: 'E said to me once ...

MINOR: 'All the words in the language finally explained. We'll understand … everything.'

COLEMAN: That was Dr. Minor. Almost 'eroic. In an 'omicidal lunatic sort of way.

(MINOR is looking through the books on his desk. He becomes agitated, comes to the door of his cell.)

MINOR: Mr. Coleman! Mr. Coleman!

COLEMAN: That didn't stop 'im being so much of a bloody nuisance I could 'ave cheerfully strangled 'im. Yes, on some days, he could even drive me to drink.

(He takes swig from hip flask and enters cell.)

Be patient, Doctor!

MINOR: They have been into my rooms! Mr. Murphy let them in again!

COLEMAN: Oh, I don't think so!

MINOR: *(Spitting.)* They have forced the metal biscuits into my mouth. I can still taste the poison coating! They have hidden my flute again and I cannot find it!

COLEMAN: Your flute always turns up eventually.

MINOR: They have tampered with my books!

COLEMAN: How do you know that?

MINOR: In a book on anatomy, one of the leaves is turned down at an illustration of the female genitalia!

COLEMAN: Wish I'd known you kept those kind of books in your library, Dr. Minor!

MINOR: They have turned down a leaf in my copy of Catullus also, at a lewd passage about a catamite.

COLEMAN: Oh? Another dirty word you're working on for the big Dictionary?

MINOR: Are those the only words you are ever interested in?

COLEMAN: I 'ave a lively, curious mind, Dr. Minor.

MINOR: You have a mind like a sewer Mr. Coleman.

COLEMAN: Doubt it runs that deep, really.

MINOR: Well what floats through it is filthy enough.

COLEMAN: Come on Dr. Minor, some words are just dirty!

MINOR: There are no dirty words Mr. Coleman. Words are pure, clean and good. They do an honest job of describing. It is the minds of men that are unclean.

COLEMAN: What's 'catamite' then?

MINOR: A boy kept for sodomite practices.

COLEMAN: Sounds like a dirty word to me! Now why'd people want to break into your cell, turn all the leaves of your books down? Don't make sense.

MINOR: They are trying to poison me. Failing that, they wish to drive me mad.

COLEMAN: Well, you mustn't let 'em drive you mad.

MINOR: I won't!

COLEMAN: That's the spirit! Don't you give in to 'em! They're only jealous!

MINOR: Jealous?

COLEMAN: Your reputation as a scholar.

MINOR: Are you humouring me, Mr. Coleman?

COLEMAN: Humouring the inmates is my job, Dr. Minor.

MINOR: Then you do it poorly. The inmate should not know he is being humoured.

COLEMAN: Thank you for 'elping me see my failings. I will endeavour to mend.

MINOR: I wish to see the Superintendent.

COLEMAN: Dr. Nicholson will 'ave no more meetings with you about men breaking into your room.

MINOR: He must see me! It is unbearable!

COLEMAN: Didn't 'e agree to the metal floor being put in? Stop them breaking in through the floorboards?

MINOR: At my expense!

COLEMAN: Even so.

MINOR: What use is the metal floor if Mr. Murphy is letting the men in through the door?

COLEMAN: Poor old Murphy gets the blame again!

MINOR: He's an Irishman, like the men who persecute me! He's in league with them!

COLEMAN: So he let them in this time to tamper with your books. Well, what if *you* turned down the leaves of these books in an absent-minded moment, years ago, and just forgot?

MINOR: Why would I do that?

COLEMAN: I don't know. Something on the pages you wanted to look at again? Difficult word for the dictionary, maybe. Like 'catamite'.

(MINOR stops pacing, appears lost in thought.)

MINOR: Years ago … You have reminded me of a time when I was capable of any depravity that money could buy and brothel supply. A time I would prefer to forget, but the mortification of being reminded may do some good. I thank you for that Mr. Coleman.

COLEMAN: Always glad to be helpful.

MINOR: Yes, it is more likely that I was marking the book myself for sordid self-gratification … The leaves here were not turned down by intruders.

COLEMAN: See? You think about these things and there's an 'armless explanation.

MINOR: Alas, my explanation is anything but … harmless.

COLEMAN: It's simpler than men coming into your cell at night.

MINOR: Yes, they did not turn the leaves down. They are not trying to drive me mad.

COLEMAN: There you are!

MINOR: No, they are simply trying to poison me.

(Pause. COLEMAN buries head in hands.)

Mr. Coleman, please bring me the scales.

COLEMAN: Oh, not the scales!

MINOR: I must weigh myself.

COLEMAN: We were gonna 'ave a break from the scales!

MINOR: It is the only way I can judge if their poison is working.

COLEMAN: The scales are very 'eavy Dr. Minor. I 'ave to carry 'em up two flights of stairs!

MINOR: *(Tearful.)* Please Mr. Coleman, I beg you. The scales!

COLEMAN: Don't upset yourself. The scales. *(Sighs.)* Go and sit down. I'll fetch 'em.

(MINOR goes and sits down on his bed, COLEMAN steps out into the corridor to address audience. Swigs from hip flask.)

Every time. Just when you were making a bit of 'eadway, scurrying back into madness like a frightened rabbit into the bushes. And then I'd get mad with 'im because 'e wouldn't let me in, and I couldn't do my job. Stupid, I know – and I know it wasn't 'is fault really. He was just frightened. And 'e'd been frightened a long time. Ever since the war.

SCENE TWO

(COLEMAN exits. Lights up on MINOR in cell.)

MINOR: Winter rains uncovered the skeletons of men who died in the previous year's battle. Two soldiers played catch with a skull. I begged respect for our fallen comrade. They laughed in my face, smashed the skull against a rock until it shattered.

We crossed Virginia into a region named 'The Wilderness', seventy square miles of hardwood trees. From the rocky heights overlooking it, green virgin forest as far as the eye could see, as if the hand of God had just made it. And very rugged – thick underbrush, ravines, few clearings except for pockets of swamp. As if Nature was trying to create one place we could not dump the filth of war. She failed.

(Distant sounds of gunfire, artillery, men's cries.)

Never this close to battle before. Men fight their way through brambles and thorns as artillery shells and explosive bullets rip them to pieces. Trees hung with human flesh drip blood on those who struggle beneath. Fires sweep through the dry brush. Our dressing stations overwhelmed; the most terrible injuries. Men blackened, burned beyond recognition, with shattered limbs and holes through their bodies who will never survive. Clawing me with sooty fingernails, 'Don't let me die, doctor! Save me ...'

Twenty-seven thousand die in two days, countless more maimed in body and mind. What do *I* do? Report the two soldiers I saw smashing the skull. 'I have *slightly* more important matters to worry about,' the senior officer drawls, a cigarette hanging from his mouth. I persist, and without looking up from his desk he says, 'Dr. Minor. Go to hell.'

(Lights change to red. Smoke drifts across stage. Battle noises louder from this point, eventually MINOR will have to shout to be heard. Walls of cell start bulging inwards in several places as if people are trying to break in. Fire glows brighter, redder.)

Many wounded lie out in the undergrowth, unable to crawl back to their lines, choking on the smoke ... roasted alive. After the screams stop ... POP! POP! Unused rifle cartridges in their belts going off in the heat. POP! A cheerful sound. Like firecrackers on the fourth of July.

Forty-eight hours awake, sawing off limbs and still a queue of men on stretchers waits to go under my knife. Trees by the field hospital catch fire. Smoke pours in, and sparks rain down on us. I look up and see soldiers advancing, like devils through the flames. Our men or theirs? I no longer care. We have turned a primeval garden into Dante's 'Inferno'. How can it ever be turned back?

On that day I fix an opinion. Despite all our culture, books, music and everything noble that humankind has ever achieved, this earth would be a better place if we had never existed.

(Crescendo of noise, GEORGE pushes his way raging through the wall of MINOR's cell.)

GEORGE: You *fucker*! You fucking *bastard*! It would be better if *you'd* never existed!

MINOR: How dare you come into my cell like this! Mr. Coleman!

GEORGE: Coleman can't 'ear you. 'E's gone home. Don't you know who I am?

MINOR: Some new devil Murphy has sent to torment me! I have never set eyes on you before!

GEORGE: Except when you shot me!

(Long pause.)

MINOR: Mr. … Merrett?

GEORGE: George Merrett. Stoker at the Red Lion Brewery. The man you murdered, you mad bastard!

MINOR: *(Stopping his ears.)* Please, enough!

GEORGE: Enough!? You fucking cunt!

MINOR: Must you use those vile words?

GEORGE: My words upset you? You fucking mad bastard! You shot me dead! You fucking killed me!

MINOR: I know I killed you. Do you have to …

GEORGE: Being killed is fucking *upsetting*!

MINOR: I thought you were someone else.

GEORGE: Who, you mad fucker? Who were you trying to shoot?

MINOR: One of the men pursuing me.

GEORGE: No one was pursuing you, you fucking nutter! You imagined it!

MINOR: An Irishman broke into my room!

GEORGE: Do I look like an Irishman!? Do I sound like a fucking Irishman!?

MINOR: I thought you broke into my room.

GEORGE: No one broke into your fucking room, you fucking lunatic!

MINOR: I chased the man down the street myself!

GEORGE: You chased me! There was no one else in the street! Two o'clock in the fucking morning! I was on my way to work. You were on your way 'ome from the fucking brothel, weren't you? That's why you liked Lambeth. Red lights, fog and fucking brothels. You chased me, I nearly got away … *(Rage subsides, he sobs brokenly.)* nearly got away. Two shots missed. I was at the corner. Frost on the cobbles. I slipped. And then, you bastard, you shot me while I was lying on the ground. I didn't 'ave a chance!

MINOR: Mr. Merrett, I would do anything to make amends.

GEORGE: Little clouds, my breath was making while I was lying there. Then it stopped, the clouds cleared, and I could see a night sky full of stars ... Why did you shoot me while I was on the ground? Even if I was a burglar? Cold-blooded, fucking murder!

MINOR: I was … in a rage, not thinking clearly.

GEORGE: My Eliza a widow, six kids left without a father because you weren't thinking clearly!

MINOR: You have no idea! They follow me! Break into my room at night! No respite, even here!

GEORGE: Who, for fuck's sake?

MINOR: Irish rebels! Fenians!

GEORGE: What!?

MINOR: They tunnel through the floor and ceiling! Sometimes through the wall … like you.

GEORGE: I'm a fucking ghost, that's why I come through walls! Can't hurt a fly. If I could, you'd be the first to fucking know!

MINOR: They try to poison me, force metal rods into my mouth coated with cyanide!

(Pause.)

GEORGE: *(Shakes head.)* You're still as fucking mad as when you shot me! Fucking good job there's no chance of you getting out. Be shooting some other poor bastard now, wouldn't you?

MINOR: I will never hold a gun in my hand again. I have seen too much of what guns can do.

GEORGE: Eliza was expecting our seventh when you shot me. Lucky number seven we used to say. I don't even know what my seventh child was.

MINOR: I heard it was … a boy.

GEORGE: *(Sobs.)* A little boy. Never seen 'is dad. You fucking mad fucking bastard!

MINOR: Do you have to keep saying that word?

GEORGE: Which fucking word?

MINOR: *(Roars.)* I know that I am mad!

(Pause.)

GEORGE: Oh, that word. So it was mad to kill me?

MINOR: Of course. I pay the price.

GEORGE: *(Looking around.)* Don't cost that much. More like a fucking library than a cell in 'ere. What's this? Wine. And brandy?

MINOR: Bourbon.

GEORGE: *(Shakes head.)* Fuck me! Men more mad than you are rotting in ordinary prison cells.

MINOR: I do not doubt it.

GEORGE: But they're not from rich families, are they? My Eliza's struggling to bring up seven kids. You sit 'ere, readin' books, swillin' fucking bourbon, payin' other inmates to wait on you and keep your fucking rooms tidy!

MINOR: Your widow will not want. The American Embassy raised a fund … because of the shame I brought on my country, and my stepmother gave a considerable sum.

GEORGE: The embassy!? Your fucking stepmother! And what 'ave you given 'er?

MINOR: Me? I could not expect your wife to accept money from the man who murdered her husband.

GEORGE: *(Laughs.)* Not from this world, are yer?

MINOR: She would accept it?

GEORGE: No idea, 'ave you? The things she's 'ad to do for money … don't fucking worry, she'll take it!

MINOR: *(Excited.)* I can write to her, yes! Care of the American Embassy!

GEORGE: Make sure you do.

MINOR: I will! The chance to do some good!

GEORGE: Don't think it'll make everything all right, though.

MINOR: I don't think that.

GEORGE: You're still the man who killed 'er fucking husband, made our children orphans.

MINOR: I never forget.

GEORGE: Give 'er a million, you'd still be *(Jabs finger at him.)* a worthless … piece … of shit.

MINOR: *(Sadly.)* I know.

(GEORGE walks across and stands over the knife on desk.)

GEORGE: *(Laughs.)* Tell me, why do they leave a convicted, 'omicidal lunatic with a knife in his cell?

MINOR: My penknife. To cut the pages of new books.

(GEORGE picks up the knife.)

GEORGE: I shouldn't be able to do that. Either you're still dreamin', or just gone a bit more mad. What should I do with this, you reckon?

(He approaches MINOR with knife outstretched. Tense pause.)

MINOR: Open the last few pages of the book. The ones no one has read yet. Cut the patient open, find where the disease is hidden.

GEORGE: What the fuck you talking about?

MINOR: Just a medical metaphor, from an old surgeon. I used to say to the poor devils under my knife, 'Be brave man, I'm trying to save your life.' *(Beat.)* Cure me.

(GEORGE laughs, hands knife to MINOR, pats his cheek.)

GEORGE: You don't get off that easy. Put that somewhere safe. See you same time tomorrow night.

(Lights down. Exit GEORGE.)

SCENE THREE

(Lights up on ELIZA sitting with MINOR in his cell. She glares fiercely at him as he speaks. Long, awkward pauses. She does not respond to questions.)

MINOR: I hope your journey was not unpleasant? You came by train?

I can ask Mr. Coleman to bring us up some tea?

(He indicates decanters.)

Some wine, or bourbon?

Mrs. Merrett, when I wrote, never in my wildest dreams did I think you would honour me with a visit.

Perhaps you regret having come, or do not wish to stay?

If it would relieve your heart to say anything to me?

(Pause. He gets out an envelope.)

As I wrote to you, I have drawn up a cheque. I do not ask for gratitude or forgiveness. I deserve neither. But I thank you from the bottom of my heart for agreeing to accept it. You have no idea how much it will ease my pain at the evil I have done to you.

ELIZA: I don't want to ease your pain.

MINOR: I can understand that.

ELIZA: Should refuse it, shouldn't I?

MINOR: I would understand if you did.

ELIZA: Very understanding, aren't you? You know I can't afford to bloody refuse it. Give it 'ere.

(Takes envelope from MINOR and puts it in her bag.)

You talk very beautifully, Mr. Minor, for a murderer.

MINOR: I know that is what I am. But I killed your husband in a rage, when the balance of my mind was disturbed. I would do anything to make amends. I wish I had died that day in his place. Most of the time I wish I had never been born.

ELIZA: You're not the only one wishes that. Your poor mother probably wishes the same.

MINOR: My mother died when I was three years old.

ELIZA: Spared your shame at least. I'm gonna ask you
something because I promised myself I'd 'ear it from your
own lips. Why'd you kill my George?

(Pause.)

MINOR: I killed your husband because I thought he had just
broken into my lodgings. I believed him to be one of a
group of men who have persecuted me for years.

ELIZA: What men?

MINOR: Irish rebels. Fenians. They have followed me here
from America, and one of the attendants is in league
with them. At night, this attendant lets them into my cell.
They abuse me and try to make me swallow pieces of
metal coated in cyanide. They … try to make me commit
unspeakable acts.

(Pause.)

ELIZA: Mad as an 'atter, aren't you? I needed to 'ear that.
When you talk all nice, like a gentleman, then I 'ate you.
I wanted to come 'ere and find you ravin' so I could feel
sorry for you and stop breakin' my 'eart over George. I've
'ad these 'eadaches see, seven years, my 'ead pounding fit
to burst. Maybe it'll stop now.

MINOR: You have not quite understood. I know I am mad, but
the men pursuing me are real.

ELIZA: *(Pats his hand.)* Course they are. I understand that.

MINOR: You do?

ELIZA: Explain to me why they're picking on you.

MINOR: Because of something I was forced to do to one of
them in America.

ELIZA: And what was that?

MINOR: I would rather not talk about it.

ELIZA: Well, I'm telling you that you 'ave to talk about it.

MINOR: I … have to?

ELIZA: If you are to earn … my forgiveness.

(Pause. MINOR speaks distractedly, half to himself.)

MINOR: Our uncivil war. Many had not the stomach for killing brother Americans, and deserted. As regimental surgeon, I once had to punish a deserter with … branding. A young Irishman, caught fleeing into the woods, little more than a boy, poor wretch. Uniform in tatters, face dirty and bloody. They dragged him before me crying, begging. I had to take the red hot iron from the brazier, press it onto his cheek. The skin melted, stuck to the metal. That hissing sound. His screams. The smell of … burning flesh. The letter 'D' for deserter branded onto his face, forever. They pour black powder into the wound so that the brand never fades. I discovered later he was an Irish rebel, one of many in our Army at that time. Well organised, violent men, planning their war against England. I knew they would exact revenge on me. This they do, every night.

(Pause. ELIZA less angry.)

ELIZA: You tell a good story, Mr. Minor. Did you see many terrible things in the war?

MINOR: I've already said more than is fit for the hearing of a lady.

ELIZA: I drink a bit too much gin to call myself that. I won't ask you to tell me more. I can see it's upset you. It 'as 'elped me, coming 'ere. Made me feel closer to George. That sound mad?

(Pause.)

MINOR: I am a madman, and so I understand it perfectly.

ELIZA: *(Laughs.)* Was that … a joke?

MINOR: I guess it was! *(Starts to cry.)* Mrs. Merrett, I don't think I have told a joke or so much as smiled in all the seven years I have been here. God bless you!

ELIZA: I don't believe in God any more. Do you?

MINOR: I stopped believing in … redemption. And that led me to live a shameful life for many years, even before I murdered your husband.

(Pause. ELIZA less angry still.)

ELIZA: Perhaps … I'll come again. Would you like that?

(Pause.)

MINOR: That would be more than I dreamed possible!

ELIZA: I don't know. I'll see 'ow I feel. If I do, is there anythin' I could bring you? From London?

MINOR: You are too kind! … No.

ELIZA: What is it?

MINOR: There are certain special books I need. The bookshop delays posting them, despite repeated requests.

ELIZA: Write down the name of the shop and the books. I'm not promising anything, mind. What you need them for anyway?

(MINOR goes to his desk and scribbles on a piece of paper. ELIZA is looking at some of his books.)

MINOR: My work on the Oxford English Dictionary. This has become my life now, Mrs. Merrett. And there is no part of my life so dark that words have not been able to illuminate it.

ELIZA: These are all foreign. Which languages you speak then?

MINOR: I can get by in Hindi, Tamil, Burmese, some of the Chinese dialects and most European languages. But

I am proudest that I speak fluent Sinhalese.

ELIZA: What's that?

MINOR: The language of Ceylon, where I spent the first thirteen years of my life. My parents were missionaries there.

ELIZA: Say something to me …

MINOR: In Sinhalese? *(Laughs.)* Lasanaya kelloo!

ELIZA: What's that mean?

MINOR: It means 'kind lady'.

(Gives her sheet of paper. She laughs.)

ELIZA: Too kind for my own good. George said I was a soft touch, an' 'e was a good judge of people.

MINOR: He must have been, to choose such a good woman for his wife.

(Tense pause.)

ELIZA: Was it nice, Ceylon?

MINOR: The day my parents sent me away was like being expelled from the Garden of Eden.

ELIZA: Why did they do that?

MINOR: Concern about my behaviour. My moral insanity was already becoming apparent.

ELIZA: I better be going. You know, it's a shame you never met George before you killed 'im. I never really learned reading and writing, but 'e liked books. 'E'd read me stories sometimes; tell me off when I used a word wrong. Taught 'imself to read at a Library. Was teaching two of our little ones. 'E wanted 'em to 'ave a better life than 'e'd 'ad.

(MINOR starts to cry.)

Oh, don't take on. It's over now. I can see you're trying to make some amends Mr. Minor. More than most murderers ever do. Anyhow, it's a great comfort for me to meet you, and see 'ow you really are stark, staring mad.

(Pause. She holds out her hand. They shake hands and she exits. He stares after her then at his hand which he holds up to his face.)

SCENE FOUR

(Lights up on COLEMAN in corridor.)

COLEMAN: Dr. Minor seemed very 'appy that night with 'ow the visit 'ad gone.

(MINOR smells hand and puts it down his trousers.)

MINOR: Lasanaya kelloo!

COLEMAN: Sinhalese, eh?

MINOR: Language of Sin!

COLEMAN: I'm not convinced those words mean exactly what 'e told 'er. You find your flute, Dr. Minor?

MINOR: I have, thank you!

COLEMAN: I'll leave you to it then. Just off on my rounds. Good night!

MINOR: Thank you. Good night, Mr. Coleman.

(Exit COLEMAN. Dim red lighting up on cell, noises of battle start up. Fire glows redder, smoke drifts across stage. MINOR mutters to himself, imitating GEORGE's voice.)

… things she's 'ad to do for money … Lambeth. Red lights, fog and fucking brothels! Lasanaya kelloo!

(Battle noises cease abruptly. ELIZA enters through wall wearing only underwear and a large, flamboyant hat. Speaks in posh dominatrix voice.)

MINOR: Mrs. Merrett! What are you doing here? It's the middle of the night!

ELIZA: Call me Mrs. Merrett when I come to you by day. At night, I am Eliza.

MINOR: Did Mr. Murphy let you in?

ELIZA: You let me in yourself, don't you remember? I haven't washed for days. I'm dirty, Dr. Minor and I'm going to do a filthy, unspeakable thing to you. Expose your virile member!

MINOR: No!

ELIZA: Come, come Dr. Minor! You've already exposed it in every brothel in London!

(She pushes his legs apart, reaches into his trousers and pulls out a flute. She walks to the front of the stage, puts it to her mouth and faces audience.)

Name the act.

MINOR: It's unspeakable!

ELIZA: You must speak it! You must say it!

MINOR: Never!

ELIZA: William!

(Pause.)

MINOR: Fellatio!

ELIZA: Now, the etymology.

(She plays repeated pattern of ascending notes on flute. MINOR's face assumes blissful expression.)

MINOR: … From the Latin verb *fellare* meaning … to suck!

(COLEMAN enters through the wall.)

COLEMAN: Dr. Minor! What's all this then?

(ELIZA stops playing, voice reverting to normal.)

ELIZA: Mr. Coleman! 'E's making me do it again!

COLEMAN: You take the biscuit Dr. Minor! You kill poor Mr. Merrett and then you 'ave 'is missus tooting your flute!

ELIZA: Makes me say all these stupid things, like I was some kind of posh tart. 'E's disgusting!

(She throws her hat down on the floor.)

COLEMAN: Disgusting, making Mrs. Merrett say things like that!

ELIZA: 'E 'ad me up the bum last time! 'E's deprived!

COLEMAN: Depraved, Mrs. Merrett.

ELIZA: 'E's not right!

COLEMAN: 'E's certainly not. Tha's why we keep 'im locked in 'ere!

ELIZA: Look at what 'e's got me wearing. I'd never wear something like this!

COLEMAN: Why not?

ELIZA: Mr. Coleman!

COLEMAN: *(To MINOR.)* For shame, Dr. Minor!

ELIZA: Look like a bleedin' Lambeth trollop!

COLEMAN: *(To MINOR.)* Really!

(GEORGE enters through wall. Comic mood vanishes. He glares at MINOR. Goes slowly over to ELIZA and places his coat around her shoulders.)

ELIZA: Oh, Georgie!

GEORGE: It's over now, darling.

ELIZA: 'E makes me pretend I don't wash or nothing. I need a bath.

GEORGE: Go and 'ave a bath. You'll feel better.

ELIZA: It's 'im who's dirty! Filthy mind! And poxy down there, from all those whores!

(*Pause.*)

GEORGE: I'm 'ere now, angel. 'E can't touch you.

ELIZA: Will you come and wash my back? Like you used to?

GEORGE: I'd love to do that sweetheart. But I can't.

ELIZA: Oh, please, Georgie!

GEORGE: I can't, Lizzie.

ELIZA: Oh, why can't you, Georgie?

(*Pause.*)

GEORGE: (*Slowly, quietly, calmly.*) Because this mad … murdering … bastard … killed me.

(*All three turn slowly and stare. MINOR crumples.*)

MINOR: (*Whispers.*) No!

(*Lights down. Exit ELIZA and MINOR. COLEMAN goes to corridor.*)

SCENE FIVE

(*Lights up on Corridor.*)

COLEMAN: We needed 'Ome Office permission for that first visit and we all thought it would be a one off. No one could believe it when she started visiting 'im regularly. 'Er own 'usband's murderer! Some said she did it for the money, but 'e was gonna give 'er the money anyway. So the newspapers and the bishops all decided it was a miracle of Christian forgiveness. And that's what it looked like. For years, Eliza was a regular guest in the Doctor's room and this woman, 'oo couldn't read 'erself, came luggin' in these massive parcels from all the London bookshops for 'is dictionary work. I don't think it was about the money or forgiveness really. I just think Eliza Merrett didn't know what to do with 'erself. And she 'ad something in common with Dr. Minor. She was lonely. Which was why she drank. *(Smiles.)* Not that I'd know anything about that.

(He swigs from hip flask. Lights down on corridor. Lights up on cell again. ELIZA and MINOR seated at table. ELIZA wearing a fine new dress. She is drunk, MINOR is uncomfortable.)

ELIZA: 'Would madam prefer the taffeta or the crepe de chine'? I didn't 'ave a bloody clue what she was on about. 'I think I prefer the pink!' 'Just a moment, madam, I will fetch assistance.' Course, she'd gone to fetch the bleedin' manager! 'E's all smiles, but it's, "ow is madam intending to pay?' 'Madam intends to pay out of this 'ere wad of spondulicks!' I says, waves it right under 'is sniffy little nose. They 'ad to carry on treating me like Lady Muck of Lavatory Hall, even though it was killing 'em. The beauty of money, Mr. Minor. Got you to thank for that.

(Embarrassed gesture from MINOR. ELIZA drains her glass. Laughs.)

Funny stuff! Is there any more?

(She holds out glass.)

MINOR: Mrs. Merrett, don't you think …

ELIZA: *(Belches.)* I wish you kept gin in your rooms. I'm not used to Bourbon.

MINOR: Then perhaps you had better not take any more.

(ELIZA glares and draws herself up erect on chair.)

ELIZA: I'll take a little wine instead. For my digestion.

(MINOR pours her wine. She takes a large swig.)

Not easy, bein' a widow bringin' up seven children.

MINOR: I'm aware of that, Mrs. Merrett.

ELIZA: I'm not talking about money. Don't 'ave money worries any more. That would 'ave hurt George more than anythin'. 'Is murderer providing better for 'is wife and kids than 'e could. That would 'ave really 'urt 'im.

MINOR: I know.

ELIZA: No, you don't know! You never met my George! You never knew 'im!

MINOR: Of course not.

ELIZA: *(Screams.)* And you never will know 'im now, because 'e's dead! Because you bloody killed 'im!

MINOR: You have every right to be angry.

(Pause. ELIZA takes a swig and holds up glass.)

ELIZA: Seven kids screaming, playing up and no father to keep 'em in line. If not for this, I'd go stark, staring mad myself, I swear to God!

(She drains her glass. Pause.)

MINOR: Would you like more wine? Perhaps some more bourbon after all?

(Tops up her glass.)

ELIZA: It helps with the loneliness. You must understand that, sitting 'ere alone day after day?

MINOR: … Yes.

ELIZA: George always said 'the love of a good woman. That's all a man needs.' *(Laughs.)* Once 'e even said, 'e'd 'ad a few drinks, mind, 'e said, 'I'd die for you Lizzie. I'd lay down my life …' *(Starts to cry.)*

MINOR: Mrs. Merrett …

ELIZA: *(Tearful.)* I 'ave a confession, Mr. Minor. The reason I keep coming to see you is because it's the only way I can still feel close to George. Mad, eh?

MINOR: Quite mad.

ELIZA: *(Laughs.)* I'll come 'ere to visit you one day and they'll stop me on the way out and keep me inside. I wonder what 'e'd say, if 'e could see the pair of us.

(ELIZA dries her tears and smiles at MINOR.)

If 'e'd think it was wrong. Us seeing each other like this.

MINOR: Mrs. Merrett!

ELIZA: Oh 'ow long 'ave we known each other now, Mr. Minor? Call me Eliza, for God's sake!

(GEORGE enters. He glares at MINOR, ELIZA cannot see GEORGE. MINOR rushes to the door of his cell.)

MINOR: No! Mr. Coleman!

ELIZA: What's the matter?

MINOR: Coming through the walls! Mr. Coleman!

(COLEMAN enters running.)

He's here! Others will follow, swarming through the walls, down through the ceiling, forcing me to commit unspeakable acts!

COLEMAN: You'd better leave Mrs. Merrett.

ELIZA: Oh no! This is what I've come to see.

MINOR: Not even night time yet, and he's already here!

ELIZA: Who's here Mr. Minor?

MINOR: George Merrett.

ELIZA: What's he doing?

GEORGE: Keepin' a fucking eye on the mad cunt who shot 'im.

COLEMAN: Dr. Minor! Language like that in front of a lady!?

ELIZA: You think because we're labouring people that we use the language of the gutter? While you show off Dictionary words that no one understands? For your information, George 'ated bad language all his life. 'E didn't use it, and 'e never let anyone use those words in front of me or the kids. That's not 'im speaking, it's you Mr. Minor.

COLEMAN: I'm going to insist that you leave now, Mrs. Merrett.

ELIZA: I'm going. You won't see me again. My 'eadache's come back. I thought I could forgive you, but I know now I can't.

MINOR: *(Sobs.)* Am I not mad? You said so yourself. What cure is there for that?

ELIZA: You've got a choice! What choice did you give George?

MINOR: I cannot help what I am!

ELIZA: You can help it! You can *change*!

COLEMAN: Enough!

(All freeze. Lights down on cell. COLEMAN steps outside into corridor. ELIZA exits. MINOR sits down.)

SCENE SIX

(COLEMAN takes swig from hip flask.)

COLEMAN: As suddenly as she arrived, she was gone. I encouraged 'im to write and apologise for 'is filthy language that day. 'E did write, begging 'er to come back and to forgive 'im again for everything. She never replied. The money just 'elped 'er drink 'erself to death quicker. Then 'er ghost joined George's in 'is cell at night. And in 'is dreams. I was in them too sometimes, 'e said, and Murphy. When I asked 'm what we were all doing there, 'e said ...

MINOR: Helping me to understand forgiveness.

(COLEMAN exits. Red lights up on cell. ELIZA enters cell through the wall.)

ELIZA: You shot my Georgie, an' 'e bled to death on dirty cobblestones. Our son Freddie went and killed 'imself afterwards as well. I took to drink and died of liver failure. You broke my 'eart, Mr. Minor. 'Ow are you goin' to make everything better?

MINOR: Living the rest of my life without a sound night's sleep. Dreams – crawling with demons to the end.

ELIZA: That won't cheer me up! I know what you could do though – tell me a story.

(Pause.)

MINOR: A story?

ELIZA: Not about the war. I'm tired of death. Tell me about Ceylon, Mr. Minor.

MINOR: Dante says the greatest pain souls in Hell suffer is remembering happy times. I would rather not talk about it.

ELIZA: Well, I'm telling you that you 'ave to talk about it.

(Pause.)

MINOR: I … have to?

ELIZA: If you are to earn … my forgiveness.

(Pause. Lighting change. Sounds of sea crashing on beach and wheeling seagulls. They act out a scene from the island paradise.)

MINOR: We lived at the mission station near the coast.

ELIZA: Show me.

MINOR: The breeze is warm and thick with the scent of cloves and cinnamon. I go to gather fruit …

ELIZA: And the trees are covered in blossom. White …

MINOR: Yellow …

ELIZA: Purple.

MINOR: Break open coconuts ...

ELIZA: Drink the milk. Mangoes ...

MINOR: Kumquats ...

ELIZA: Passion fruits hang from the branches

MINOR: And we *gorge* ... And the sun shines

ELIZA: ... Forever. Tell me about the beach.

(Sound of children running, laughing, splashing.)

MINOR: I am thirteen, and although forbidden, I go to watch the native children.

ELIZA: Boys and girls your own age and older running through the waves ...

MINOR: No more aware of their naked parts than of the blossoms in their hair.

ELIZA: Graceful stalk ...

MINOR: Delicate bud ...

ELIZA: Soft flower.

MINOR: They invite me to join them and we chase each other.

ELIZA: Kisses salted with seawater ...

MINOR: Sweat glistening on our skin.

ELIZA: The world is young.

MINOR: There is no such thing as shame.

(Pause.)

ELIZA: And?

MINOR: The rest is ... unspeakable.

ELIZA: You must speak it! What did I bring you all them books for? Come on, Dictionary man!

(Pause. MINOR speaks slowly and quietly.)

MINOR: Fellatio. Cunnilingus. Masturbation. Intercourse. Buggery.

(COLEMAN enters.)

COLEMAN: That all happened on *one beach*? That's 'alf the dirty words in the Dictionary!

ELIZA: Shut up, Mr. Coleman!

COLEMAN: Makes the Monkey Boy of Madagascar seem tame!

ELIZA: You 'aven't finished yet, 'ave you? William?

MINOR: There's no more to say.

(Pause. ELIZA is looking out over audience's heads.)

ELIZA: What about the man on the beach. American? No – 'e's *Irish*. Soldier? No – a *missionary*. The other children have all run off. Maybe they know him?

MINOR: No!

(MINOR pulls out a gun and points it at her.)

COLEMAN: Dr. Minor! We 'ave a *very* clear policy on firearms at Broadmoor! Give me that gun at once!

(MINOR points gun at him and he quickly draws back.)

All right! Keep the gun! Just don't point it at me!

MINOR: Mr. Murphy!

COLEMAN: Murphy won't 'elp. 'E's the one 'oo let us all in!

ELIZA: You're getting confused, Mr. Minor.

MINOR: Do you bring the poisoned rods to force into my mouth?

COLEMAN: *(Sighs.)* I think the rabbit 'as bolted. You won't escape by being mad, Dr. Minor.

ELIZA: You'll only 'ave to go through it all again. Don't you want it to stop?

MINOR: I can never leave.

ELIZA: You can leave anytime. We 'ave the key.

COLEMAN: *(Jangling keys.)* Right 'ere.

ELIZA: You can choose not to be mad, William. You've got a *choice*! You can *change*!

MINOR: *(Shouts.)* I cannot! I will not!

ELIZA: Trouble is, you 'ad no gun when the man led you away from the beach, did you? Where did 'e lead you, William? You said that words could illuminate. Shine them now. Into the darkness. Let us 'elp.

MINOR: No!

ELIZA: Fellatio?

COLEMAN: Masturbation?

ELIZA: Buggery?

(MINOR points the gun at each of them in turn. Long pause. The truth, at last, has come out.)

ELIZA: *(Nods.)* Buggery.

COLEMAN: *(Nods.)* Masturbation.

ELIZA: *(Nods.)* Fellatio.

(MINOR rushes to door of cell.)

MINOR: Mr. Murphy!

COLEMAN: What was that word? I could never remember it.

ELIZA: We're your friends, William.

MINOR: I have no friends.

COLEMAN: *Catamite*! That was it!

(Bright red lights up on stage. Sounds of battle in background. Fog starts to drift across stage. GEORGE enters through the wall. The three characters circle MINOR.)

GEORGE: The man leads me into the wilderness where rotting flesh hangs from the trees in place of blossom. The undergrowth is a tangle of maggots and amputated human arms. Fingers claw and scratch my legs with bleeding, blackened nails. Everywhere, the stomach – wrenching stench of … mortality.

COLEMAN: The only light is from burning bushes and trees. The sun never shines; continual rain uncovers more and more skeletons under the soil. Men with holes right through their bodies beg me to save them. When I cannot, they curse me with their dying breath in that filthy Irish brogue.

ELIZA: I want to do good, but instead I saw off limbs and press red-hot irons onto flesh while men scream abuse at me. To be a doctor was the only thing I ever wanted, but my puny efforts to save life are buried under an avalanche of death.

GEORGE: *(Strong Irish Accent.)* 'I am going to show you something' …

ELIZA: The man says to me as he leads me away from the beach …

GEORGE: 'I am going to explain something to you.' And he shows me the meaning of … *helplessness.*

(ELIZA walks slowly towards MINOR. COLEMAN is watching the fog. Battle sounds louder.)

ELIZA: Give me the gun.

COLEMAN: Bad feeling about this.

MINOR: Get back!

GEORGE: Three shots … a foggy night in Lambeth.

COLEMAN: Oh dear …

ELIZA: It won't 'elp. It never 'elps.

(*MINOR shoots the other three. As he does, GEORGE and ELIZA exit and COLEMAN goes and sits back in corridor, reading his penny dreadful. Battle sounds throughout.*)

Just means we 'ave to start all over again.

SCENE SEVEN

(*Battle sounds cease abruptly. MINOR looks through books on his desk. Comes to cell door.*)

MINOR: Mr. Coleman!

(*COLEMAN takes swig from hip flask.*)

COLEMAN: Be patient, Doctor!

MINOR: Mr. Coleman!

(*COLEMAN takes swig from hip flask and enters cell.*)

COLEMAN: Yes, I know! They've been into your rooms! They've been tamperin' with your books! Mr. Murphy let them in!

MINOR: No. Not Mr. Murphy. Last night I pretended to be asleep and I heard my cell door opening. Then I saw you come in and move things around my room and hide my flute.

(*Pause. COLEMAN is silent, possibly tearful.*)

Are you unhappy, Mr. Coleman?

COLEMAN: Last night was the first time I've ever done anything like this. I don't know why I did it. I'm sorry Dr. Minor, I truly am. Would you like to report the matter to Dr. Nicholson?

MINOR: I don't think so. But after you left, I had a particularly difficult night. I wonder if I could trouble you to bring me the scales?

COLEMAN: Of course.

(He makes to exit and MINOR calls after him.)

MINOR: Mr. Coleman, if it is any consolation, I forgive you.

COLEMAN: I don't deserve it.

MINOR: Who among us ever does?

COLEMAN: Thank you.

(MINOR exits. Lights up on COLEMAN in corridor. He takes out hip flask and empties it onto stage.)

And I 'aven't touched a drop since. Don't know 'ow long it'll last this time, but I terrified myself that night. What else was I capable of? I was ashamed and I couldn't believe what I'd done, but I think 'e'd worn me down. There was just no end to all 'is misery and guilt. I ended up being angry with 'im because I couldn't help 'im. After Eliza died 'e started readin' a lot of theological books to 'elp with the dictionary work and that made the nightmares even worse. Every sinning part of 'im 'ad to be punished, 'e said. Birds came to peck out 'is eyes, and poisoned food was funnelled into 'is mouth and devils smashed 'is 'ands with 'ammers. 'E'd show me the scratched eyes and bleeding fingernails too, but once, I saw him slam the door on his own fingers till the nails cracked and bled. Yeah, every evil part had to be punished. And that's what brought us to the third of December, 1902.

(COLEMAN sits down again and starts reading magazine. Lights up on cell, enter MINOR from back of cell, his trousers drenched in blood down to the knees. He holds a bloodstained penknife in one hand, in the other, something audience do not see at first. He stands before cell door.)

MINOR: *(Whispers.)* Behold, I show you a mystery. We shall not all die, but we shall be *changed. (Calmly, to COLEMAN.)* Mr. Coleman, you had better send for the medical officer at once. I have injured myself.

(MINOR drops penknife to ground, opens other hand, holds up his severed penis and considers carefully. Slowly squeezes it and blood drips onto the floor. Shocked pause. Throws it into fire. COLEMAN still reading, speaks without looking.)

COLEMAN: Oh, not again, Dr. Minor! You'll 'ave no fingernails left at this rate!

(Continues reading for a few moments. Finally gets up reluctantly and goes to cell door. Sees MINOR.)

MINOR: Mr. Coleman, do you know the word for the surgical amputation of the penis? *Peotomy*! Words are not dirty, they are the clean, sharp knives that the surgeon uses to do his work. Cut off the diseased member, that the patient may live! *Peotomy*!

COLEMAN: Jesus Christ!

(COLEMAN shouts offstage.)

Mr. Murphy! Fetch the Super! Quick!

(He helps MINOR to lie on floor, supporting him.)

You'll be all right Doctor. Try to stay awake! You'll need something to stop the bleedin'.

MINOR: There will not be much more bleeding. I tied a ligature around the base before I cut it off. I will go into shock now, Mr. Coleman. This should not give cause for concern. The body's natural response to traumatic injury. I saw it many times on the battlefield and after amputations.

(MINOR shaking. COLEMAN tries to steady him.)

COLEMAN: What did you … do with it?

MINOR: We may return to the garden at last, for it has been purified. The snake has been cast into the flames.

COLEMAN: *(Whispers.)* Christ!

(MINOR closes his eyes.)

Dr. Minor! Don't die on me, for God's sake! 'Elp is on its way!

(Cradles MINOR very tenderly, speaks tearfully.)

You 'ang on. You're gonna be all right. You're goin' to get better.

MINOR: *(Murmurs.)* I will be … *better.*

COLEMAN: You will.

(MINOR rouses and speaks with great effort.)

MINOR: I will probably lose consciousness now. This is quite normal and should not give rise to alarm. Everything … is … quite … *normal …*

(Eyes close and body goes limp in COLEMAN's arms.)

COLEMAN: *(Whispers.)* Doctor Minor? Doctor Minor!

(Blackout. Exit MINOR. Lights up on COLEMAN in corridor. He holds up penny dreadful.)

A bit they missed out! And the story don't make sense without it. But it didn't kill 'im. Surgeon see, knew what 'e was doing. Out of 'ospital within a month and lived another eighteen years! Was eventually allowed out and back to America. That's where his story ended. 1910. The Retreat 'ospital for the elderly insane, 'artford, Connecticut. Dribblin', ravin', strikin' fellow patients. Did the pen knife 'elp? Difficult to say, but 'ow many of us try that 'ard to be a better person? 'Eroic. In an 'omicidal lunatic sort of way.

That battlefield in Virginia – Doctor Minor was wrong, you know. They never destroyed the wilderness. Rain washed the blood and ashes away, the dead went into the earth, the trees all grew back. It's peaceful now and beautiful again. There's a museum an' a memorial cemetery, an' a man taking tours round 'oo'll tell you the story of everything that 'appened.

(Lights dim to black.)